10 Years of Haus Publishing
Publisher's Note

In January 2003 we published our first book, a masterfully insightful biography of the legendary Winston Churchill by Sebastian Haffner. A German exile's homage to his adopted homeland seemed a fitting first publication for a London publisher and historian of German descent. The edition you hold in your hands is in other words not just a good thing in itself, but marks our ten-year anniversary.

There is no doubt that we're a small publisher. But how small is 'small'? For several years we operated from my loft, and even today the offices above our bookshop, the bookHaus, off Sloane Square, are of a cellular rather than expansive nature. Yet in ten years we have been responsible for publishing some 600 editions. They include works of fiction, history and biography, as well as visual art and earth science. There are numerous international co-editions and new translations of works previously unseen in English, not to mention our many original commissions. Such is the diversity of our list that I am often asked whether there's a common theme, a Haus style. To better answer this, I defer to an excerpt from this book:

> 'No one will ever understand the phenomenon that was Churchill by regarding him simply as a politician and statesman who was ultimately destined, like Asquith or Lloyd George, Wilson or Roosevelt, to conduct a war. Nor was he a politician who had somehow to prove himself in war; he was a warrior who realized that politics forms part of the conduct of war … To classify him correctly, we must think of other, older names: Gustavus Adolphus, Cromwell, Prince Eugene, Frederick the Great, Napoleon …'

Quintessential Haffner, no doubt, but I'd like to think of this as quintessential Haus too: crisp, wide-ranging, historically aware, entranced by the making of the 20th century, but with an international perspective that a British author might lack.

If one were to select five books that represent us – not only five of the best, but five types – then *Churchill* must be one of them. Immediately, this book on Churchill brings to my mind our biography *Gandhi* (2007), written by his grandson, Rajmohan Gandhi. I'm sure Churchill would have been horrified at my pairing him with the 'seditious Inner Temple lawyer', yet the parallel is irresistible. There is the same paradox of personality, the same sense of destiny.

If I think of something we have endeavoured to make our own, it would be the original book series; exemplified by our 20-volume *20 Prime Ministers of the 20th Century* and more recently, *The Makers of the Modern World*, a collection of 32 studies of the background to and participants in the Paris Peace Conference. A perfect distillation of the latter project is the single volume *Makers of the Middle East* (2011), which brings together the original volumes on Emir Faisal, Mustafa Kemal (or 'Atatürk'), and Chaim Weizmann, in a unified text.

Which provides me with an all too convenient link to our Arabia Books imprint, which has, since 2008, seen us become one of the world's principal publishers of Arabic fiction in translation. That alone is an extraordinary fact, but it is fiction like Rafik Schami's *The Dark Side of Love* (2009) that is more extraordinary still, not only in its epic re-imagining of the modern history of Syria and its neighbours in piercingly personal terms, but also in its pedigree – from the Arab mind, into the German language, and on into English, via the pitch-perfect translation of Anthea Bell.

Our Haus, as must be clear by now, has many rooms. My mother Ilse, as commissioning editor and co-publisher, has expanded our initial idea of the Armchair Traveller into a fine library of 96 diverse volumes of exceptional travel writing. Take one representative of her series: *The Golden Step* (2007). In this book Christopher Somerville sets out to walk the length of Crete: a journey, I remember thinking when I first read it, that bore some resemblance to that of the independent publisher – alone, on a road that may be no more than a rumour, and all the while beset by hungry, aggressive predators!

As with all new ventures, our first years of publishing were a steep learning curve, but I simply took the view: 'why not?' Some publishers might have been more inclined to ask 'why?', than 'why not?', but I hope we at Haus have tapped into a source of optimistic energy that is not exactly English – or is it? Once again I'll refer to Churchill, for many the epitome of an Englishman: 'inactivity was Winston Churchill's personal hell,' says Haffner. And so it is with us. Whatever we have planned for the future, I can guarantee you there is unlikely to be much in the way of inactivity!

Barbara Haus Schwepcke
London, January 2013

Churchill

Sebastian Haffner

translated by John Brownjohn
introduced by Peter Hennessy

HAUS PUBLISHING · LONDON

Originally published under the title *Winston Churchill*
in the series "rowohlts monographien"

Copyright © 1967 by Rowohlt Taschenbuch Verlag GmbH,
Reinbek bei Hamburg

Copyright © 2001 by Kindler Verlag GmbH, Berlin

This English translation first published in Great Britain in 2003 by
Haus Publishing Ltd, 70 Cadogan Place, London SW1X 9AH

This edition published in 2013

English translation © John Brownjohn 2003, 2012
Introduction © Peter Hennessy 2003, 2012

The moral right of the authors has been asserted

A CIP catalogue record for this book is available from the British Library

ISBN 978-1908323-37-8

Printed and bound in Germany by
fgb · freiburger graphische betribe
www.fgb.de

Contents

Introduction

Sebastian Haffner brought a cultivated and sharp yet scholarly Central European eye to mid-twentieth-century Britain, whence the high tide of fascist totalitarianism had decanted him in time to savour Winston Churchill's dramatic ascent to political, historical, and global immortality. His real name was Raimund Pretzel but, once he took up his anti-Hitler pen in Britain, a cover needed to be invented to protect relatives still living in Germany. His new pseudonym fused the middle name of J S Bach and the Symphony No 35 of Mozart.

Haffner blended brio and insight on the pages of his books and the newspapers for which he wrote. He was, for example, one of the very first exponents of the new 'profile' genre pioneered by his friend, patron, and editor at the *Observer*, David Astor, during the Second World War. Just listen to Haffner the conservative, intellectual democrat in his famous 'profile' of Hitler which appeared in the *Observer* in May 1942 almost three years to the day before the empire of the 'the crank', as Haffner called him, went down to final ruin:

> The crank in his unhappy youth knocked at many doors; and was always refused ... This period lasted for several years; it was a unique experience for a future statesman ... He divined that the mentality of the crowd is not the sum total of the mentality of the individuals which form it, but their lowest common denominator: that their intellectual

powers are not integrated by contact but bewildered by the interference for their minds – light plus light resulting in darkness; that their emotional vibrations, however, increase by induction and self-induction like the current in a wire coil. By descending into the bottom strata of society the crank made the discovery of his life: the discovery of the lowest common denominator. The master key was found.

In short, Haffner was a connoisseur of the two great duellists of 1940 when, as he puts it in this volume, thanks to Churchill's ascent to its premiership, 'Britain threw herself in the path of Hitler's breakthrough at the crucial moment, when his triumph was almost complete.' With a journalist's economy with words and an artist's sweep across a broad canvas, Haffner characteristically rounds off this paragraph by observing that such a policy was 'strictly speaking' against Britain's interests 'since she risked not only her physical existence but the basis of her economic and imperial existence as well. In the event, she successfully preserved her physical existence but lastingly ruined her economy and lost her empire.'

Haffner had a gift for capturing episode, personality, and context in paragraphs brimming with content. He was plainly fascinated both by British history and the glorious anachronism 'of a born grand seigneur' leading a coalition of all parties (including several men of the Labour Movement, such as Ernest Bevin, with whom he got on famously well) in the late spring, summer, and Battle of Britain autumn of 1940. Haffner describes this defining moment as 'a rigorous examination to which destiny – with which he maintained an old, intimate, atavistically religious relationship – had submitted his mental fibre before finally disclosing what it had in mind for him; before finally giving him his head, finally permitting him to show what he was made of and what he could do.'

Haffner is as vivid on Churchill the Edwardian 'New Liberal' and on Churchill the grand old man in his early 1950s twilight premiership – attempting one last heave to ease the Cold War before the dreadful new hydrogen weapons scorched and contaminated the world – as he is on the man of destiny in 1940 around whom geopolitics revolved as Britain made its last throw as a superpower. There is not a dull page or a stale metaphor in the book.

The library shelves groan with studies of Churchill. Compared to most, Haffner's book is slim, fast-paced, and written with the body barely cold. It can, however, be read with great pleasure, profit, and speed without the slightest danger of tiring grey cells or arms. The mind behind it, to adapt a phrase of Bryan Magee's, was provincial neither in time nor in place. Churchill welcomed the victims of the axis powers to the last great European capital to hold out against them. Haffner repaid his personal debt most handsomely within these pages.

PETER HENNESSY
Attlee Professor of Contemporary British History
Queen Mary, University of London

Churchill as a young parliamentarian in the Lower House in 1900

Father and Son · 1874–1895

The components of the name Churchill, 'church' and 'hill', are suggestive of the English countryside. And, indeed, the Churchills were country gentlefolk from the south-west of England until a branch of the family was elevated to the nobility at the dawn of the eighteenth century. This was thanks to an extraordinary scion of the family, who was born John Churchill in 1650 but died the Duke of Marlborough in 1722. Courtier and genius, diplomat and traitor, general and statesman, he might have sprung from the pages of one of Shakespeare's historical plays.

At the height of his career, Marlborough was the heart and soul of the great European coalition that broke the supremacy of the French king Louis XIV (1638–1715), and which history books drily and rather disparagingly call the War of Spanish Succession (1702–13). It might almost be described as a Churchill family affair. John Churchill, Duke of Marlborough, forged the coalition and held it together, conducting the war not only politically but – at the side of Prince Eugene – militarily as well; his brother George Churchill commanded the English fleet; his brother Charles Churchill was his ablest military subordinate; and the most brilliant general on the other side, James Fitzjames, Duke of Berwick and Marshal of France, was also a Churchill, being the illegitimate son of Arabella Churchill, Marlborough's own sister, by the last Stuart king, James II (1633–1701).

However, this explosion of military talent seemed to drain

THE CHURCHILL FAMILY

the family of its vitality for a long time to come. Although the Churchills now belonged to the senior nobility – the few hundred families who owned and governed Britain – none of them left his mark on British history for the next 150 years. It was not until the 1880s that another Churchill burst upon the scene – 'like a meteor', as his contemporaries never tired of saying. This was Lord Randolph Churchill (1849–95), third son of the seventh Duke of Marlborough and father of Winston.

Lord Randolph's brief, resplendent, and grotesquely tragic career overshadowed his son's life in more ways than one, and any biography of Winston Churchill must take his father's career as its starting point.

Lord Randolph had one trait in common with his illustrious forebear: a quick and brilliantly intuitive cast of mind. He was the first Churchill since the Duke of Marlborough to possess genius, but a genius of the kind that in many overbred families coincides with the growth of decadence. Despite a profoundly passionate nature, Marlborough had been extraordinarily self-disciplined, engagingly courteous, coolly charming, patient, deliberate, and almost super-human in his perseverance. Lord Randolph was the complete opposite: on the one hand unbridled, overbearing, disdainful, and offensive to the point of rudeness; on the other, vulnerable in the extreme, warm-hearted, quixotically chivalrous, and reckless to a degree that aroused admiration in some but caused many to doubt his sanity. At the height of his brief renown, for example, the elderly Queen Victoria (1819 –1901) quite seriously and spitefully described him as a madman – and he was, in fact, mentally deranged when he died at the age of only 45.

At 24, after graduating from Oxford with an excellent degree, he went off to France and loafed around while waiting to stand for Parliament at the next general election. There he met Jennie Jerome, one of the century's great beauties, an American girl of

Franco-Scottish descent enriched with a dash of Native American blood. They were engaged within 48 hours of meeting. Her father was an astute but nouveau riche and eccentric New York millionaire who was well aware of the aversion 'the English have against Americans socially'. He was right. Lord Randolph's parents were horrified by the proposed match and wrote to him 'You must allow it is slightly coming down in pride for us to contemplate the connection.' Six months later the young couple married nevertheless – at the registry office in the British embassy in Paris. Lord Randolph's parents did not attend, but sent a letter of grudging approval: 'She is one whom you have chosen with less than usual deliberation.'

A mere seven months later their first son was born in the ladies' cloakroom at Blenheim Palace, the magnificently regal residence erected as a monument to the Battle of Blenheim (1704) by the great Marlborough. Having insisted on being invited to a ball there despite her advanced state of pregnancy, Jennie was assailed by labour pains while dancing. She left the ballroom and made for her bedroom by way of 'the longest corridor in Europe', but got no further than the cloakroom. There, amid velvet muffs, fur coats and plumed hats, she had a precipitate delivery. It was 30 November 1874, and Winston Leonard Spencer Churchill was born.

Eighteen months later the beau monde of London was rocked by a scandal centred on Lord Randolph. It involved a high-born married woman who had been the mistress first of the Prince of Wales (later Edward VII) and then of Lord Randolph's elder brother, the Marquess of Blandford. Highly aggrieved, the Prince posed as a champion of decorum and morality: he declared that both parties should divorce and that Blandford should marry the lady in question. Lord Randolph sprang to his brother's defence and publicly declared that a divorce case would inevitably bring to light certain letters that had 'escaped His Royal Highness's pen and recollection'.

THE BIRTH OF WINSTON

An aristocratic childhood. Churchill in his sailor suit aged six in 1881

The Prince of Wales thereupon challenged him to a duel. Lord Randolph offered to fight any representative the Prince cared to name; he could not, however, take up arms against his future sovereign. The Prince retorted that he would never again enter any house that received the Churchills. The Prime Minister, shrewd old Benjamin Disraeli, now took a hand in the matter. He persuaded the Duke of Marlborough to go to Ireland as Lord Lieutenant, taking his unruly son along as his private secretary. The Duke, who had previously declined the viceregal post because of the immense expenditure it entailed, reluctantly acquiesced. The Churchills went into splendid exile, with the result that young Winston's earliest memories were of Ireland – of the fearsome Fenians, of parades and assassinations, and of a theatre that was burnt down while he was enjoying a children's performance.

Lord Randolph became a politician in Ireland. He had previously been what would now be termed a playboy, but Ireland awakened his political instincts. When he returned to London in 1879, aged 30, and resumed his seat in the

Benjamin Disraeli (1804–81) and William Ewart Gladstone (1809–98) were the two great British prime ministers of the nineteenth century. Disraeli held the office twice (1868 and 1874–80), representing the Conservative Party, while Gladstone, representing the Liberals, held it four times (1868–74, 1880–5, 1886 and 1892–4). Between them they dominated Victorian politics and set the agenda for Britain's era of imperial grandeur.

House of Commons, he brought with him something possessed by no other British politician of his day. It is a concept on which all the conservative parties of Europe subsist even now: 'Tory democracy'.

To most people, the rise of democracy seemed to betoken the demise of any party rooted in aristocracy and tradition, and the English Conservatives in 1880 were sunk in gloom. Disraeli, the old magician, had resigned and William Gladstone, the great Liberal, was Prime Minister once more. Thanks to his policy of progressively widening of the franchise – miners and day labourers now had the vote; an outrageous state of affairs! – Gladstone seemed capable of steadily undermining the Conservatives, the party of aristocratic wealth and privilege, and transforming the Liberals, the bourgeois party of progress and reform, into the permanent party of government. Why should miners and labourers – even, one day, factory workers – ever vote Conservative? The only person to entertain that possibility was crazy Lord Randolph Churchill.

Churchill (*right*) with his mother Jennie and brother Jack

In this instance, however, he was far-sighted rather than crazy. He discerned that liberalism was a fundamentally middle-class movement, and that the proletarian, uneducated, vulnerable masses to whom it had granted the vote could readily be converted into an electoral reservoir by a party composed of self-assured gentlemen who knew how to impress them and were not too proud to woo and bribe them with the aid of demagogy – but also with a genuine understanding of their needs. Lord Randolph's political ideas combined Bonapartist echoes and foretastes of Fascism with genuine *noblesse oblige* (privilege entails responsibility), and it is hard, even now, to distinguish between the genuine and false notes in his speeches. He was a demagogue of the first order. The surprising thing is that he was also a truly perceptive politician.

It took Lord Randolph Churchill only six years – the period between 1880 and 1886 – to make the Conservatives the party of government once more. It was to remain so for another two decades. In the process he became the most famous and popular, but also the most caricatured and hated, politician in England.

Hated, yes, but not only by the Liberals, whom he attacked and harried with a ferocity, brutality, and savage wit unprecedented in English public life. The leaders of his own party – patriarchal, aristocratic, upright, and starchy men – also viewed his wild antics on their behalf with faint distaste and unease. Lord Randolph responded in kind with undisguised contempt.

Once he had become politically indispensable, he took to enforcing his every wish by grandly threatening to resign. Despite this, when Lord Salisbury entered upon his long premiership in 1886, he made the madman to whom he owed it his second in command by appointing him Chancellor of the Exchequer and Leader of the House of Commons – in effect, vice-premier. That was in August 1886. In December Lord Randolph resigned all of his posts and was politically a dead man from then

Robert Gascoyne Cecil (1830–1903), 3rd Marquess of Salisbury, was Prime Minister in 1885–6, 1886–92 and 1895–1902. The embodiment of the Conservative Party's dominance of late-Victorian politics, he was suspicious of the populism of his predecessor, Disraeli, and of Randolph Churchill. His period of office saw a return to a more traditional concept of Conservatism, including support for the Anglican Established Church, maintenance of law and order and property rights, and a resolute defence of British interests abroad.

on. It was the most sudden, thorough and gratuitous act of political suicide in British political history.

The reason for Lord Randolph's resignation was trivial: a dispute over the army budget such as often occurs between ministers of war and finance. However, Lord Randolph had, in his arrogant way, become unused to waging such battles patiently and was accustomed to settling them by threatening to resign. He may well have intended to do the same on this occasion, and was surprised when his resignation was summarily accepted.

The circumstances were most unusual. He penned his letter of resignation at Windsor Castle, after an audience with the Queen and on her own royal notepaper (something for which she never forgave him). He also went to the trouble of driving to the editorial offices of *The Times* and ensuring that the news appeared in next morning's edition, hot off the press. He did not even tell his wife. He simply held out the front page with the words: 'A surprise for you.'

Perhaps Queen Victoria was right when she called him mentally deranged. Perhaps he really was suffering from an euphoric, preliminary onset of the paralytic collapse that became manifest a few years later and eventually finished him off just short of his forty-sixth birthday. But this no more accounts for – or debases – the grotesque magnificence of his disdainful throwaway gesture than does the roughly contemporaneous *Thus Spake Zarathustra* of the German philosopher Friedrich Nietzsche (1844–1900), whose own insanity was also looming. Illness may intensify genius and character to a weird, uncanny extent, but it does not create them. It all depends on the nature of the invalid.

He who discards the world has lost it for ever. One grand gesture, and everything is over; no renewed ascent is possible. As one contemporary put it: 'He has thrown himself from the top of the ladder, and will never reach it again!' Lord Randolph had made himself redundant; there was nothing really left for him to do in England. He went on world tours that bored him, wrote well-paid but mediocre newspaper articles, and essayed a hopeless political comeback which did no more than painfully expose his incipient decline. It would be better to draw a veil over Lord Randolph Churchill's last, sad years.

Yet those years provided a form of consolation that he failed to notice. Amid the smug *schadenfreude* that accompanied his fall, amid all the shoulder-shrugging, the universal rejection, and eventually – that ultimate humiliation – the burgeoning pity directed at him, the fallen idol retained one ardent admirer, supporter, and disciple: his young son Winston. He paid no heed to this fact and derived no solace from it; on the contrary, it added to the bitterness of his latter years that this son was, in his eyes, an untalented, hopeless failure. Conversely, Lord Randolph's disregard helped to poison his son's early years, which were dismal enough in any case.

Winston Churchill later wrote about his boyhood and adolescence, the period bounded by his seventh and nineteenth birthdays:

In retrospect these years form not only the least agreeable, but the only barren and unhappy period of my life. I was happy as a child with my toys in my nursery. I have been happier every year since I became a man. But this interlude of school makes a sombre grey patch upon the chart of my journey. It was an unending spell of worries that did not then seem petty, and of toil uncheered by fruition; a time of discomfort, restriction and purposeless monotony.

What he himself did not see, but what the remote observer can clearly discern, is that these were also years of struggle – indeed, the hardest years of a life full of struggle: years during which he waged an utterly hopeless, quite unwinnable but never abandoned battle. As a boy, Churchill refused to surrender to the all-powerful, overarching educational machine to which he was subjected. He defied it, and was terribly mauled by it in consequence. He derived no benefit from his long and expensive education, unless one accounts it an asset that he learned, cruelly early in life, to withstand overwhelming pressure without cracking. It is commonly said that the English don't pamper their children. Like many generalizations about 'the English', this applies mainly to the English upper class, but it holds good to this day, and was even more applicable during the years when that class was still in the ascendant and little Winston Churchill grew up.

The upper class had no time for family life. A child got to know its parents in adulthood, not before. At the age of one month, the baby was handed over to its nursemaid, who henceforth replaced its mother. Winston Churchill's nurse, Mrs Everest, loved him dearly. Later on, when she visited him at his public school in her little bonnet, he embraced her in front of all his classmates – an act of extreme moral courage. He was with her when she died – by then he was a 20-year-old hussar lieutenant – and was seen to weep at her funeral. As Prime Minister during the Second World War he kept a picture of her on the wall of his study.

At four or five a boy acquired a governess who gave him his first lessons. At seven he went off to preparatory school, at thirteen to public school. Both types of schooling combined the hell of flogging with the heaven of male camaraderie, and both were quite deliberately geared to breaking their pupils' spirits before gluing them together again in a different way. By the time the alumni of these famous English schools went to Oxford or Cambridge at 18 or 19, they all possessed a standardized second personality, not unattractive but artificial, like pollarded trees in a French baroque garden. At 21 or 22 they embarked on life, made their parents' acquaintance (if all went well), and were ready to impress the world, to despise it in a very special way, and, if suitably talented, to rule it.

This educational system was well-tried and seldom failed. Its constraints were potent and redoubtable, its powers of persuasion almost irresistible. Although it destroyed the odd individual, most boys withstood its rigours and became more or less willing to be more or less completely moulded and shaped by it. Later on they looked back on their schooldays as the happiest time of their life.

Why did young Churchill resist? Why did he put up a hopeless fight against almost irresistible coercion? The only answer is, simply because it *was* coercion. *My teachers,* he wrote later, *had large resources of compulsion at their disposal. Where my reason, imagination or interest were not engaged, I would not or I could not learn. In all the twelve years I was at school no one ever succeeded in making me write a Latin verse or learn any Greek except the alphabet.* And elsewhere: *I had an innate prejudice against Latin which seemed to close my mind against it.*

Why especially against Latin? Many aspects of Churchill's bleak schooldays can only be guessed at, but in this case we possess his own account of his first Latin lesson. He was seven years old, and his mother had just dropped him off at St George's, Ascot, the leading prep school where he was to board from now on. He was taken into a Form Room and told to sit at a desk. The Form Master produced a thin, green-brown book and said: 'This is a Latin grammar. You must learn this. I will come back in half an hour and see what you know.'

Behold me then on a gloomy evening, wrote Churchill, *with an aching heart, seated in front of the First Declension.*

Mensa	*a table*
Mensa	*O table*
Mensam	*a table*
Mensae	*of a table*
Mensae	*to or for a table*
Mensa	*by, with or from a table*

It seemed like absolute nonsense to the boy, but he repeated it word-perfect to the Form Master on his return. Emboldened, Churchill asked what it meant.

'*It means what it says. Mensa, a table. Mensa is a noun of the First*

Declension. There are five declensions. You have learnt the singular of the First Declension.'

'But,' I repeated, 'what does it mean?'

'Mensa means a table,' he answered.

'Then why does mensa also mean O table,' I enquired, 'and what does O table mean?'

'Mensa, O table, is the vocative case,' he replied.

'But why O table?' I persisted in genuine curiosity.

'O table – you would use that in addressing a table, in invoking a table.' And then, seeing he was not carrying me with him, 'You would use it in speaking to a table.'

'But I never do,' I blurted out in honest amazement.

'If you are impertinent, you will be punished, and punished, let me tell you, very severely,' was his conclusive rejoinder.

Churchill reminds us that flogging with the birch in accordance with the Eton fashion was a great feature in St George's curriculum. But I am sure no Eton boy, and certainly no Harrow boy of my day, ever received such a cruel flogging as this Headmaster was accustomed to inflict upon the little boys in his care and power. They exceeded in severity anything that would be tolerated in any of the reformatories under the Home Office. My reading in later life has supplied me with some possible explanations of his temperament.

Churchill was seven when he went to St George's, and he remained there for two years. He learnt nothing. He was brutally beaten again and again but still learnt nothing. He stamped on the headmaster's straw hat in protest one day (with predictable results). He developed a lisp and a stammer. His parents, who noticed nothing when he came home for the holidays, kept sending him back to this hell on earth for two long years. Finally, when he was just short of nine, his health gave way. Alarmed, his parents sent him to another school in Brighton – for a dose of good sea air.

The Brighton school, though slightly less prestigious and rather less strict, was cast in much the same mould. In any case, the damage was done. Young Churchill learnt nothing at Brighton either, nor did he later at Harrow, which should not by rights have accepted him. He handed in blank sheets after sitting the entrance examination in Latin and mathematics, but the headmaster felt he could hardly reject the son of the illustrious Lord Randolph Churchill. At Harrow Winston was an eternal repeater. English was the only subject at which he excelled, his mind being 'closed' to anything else. He was also an unrepentant failure at school sports. He detested cricket and football as heartily as Latin and mathematics, and he made no friends. He had clearly set his heart against the constraints and conventions of school life. He was inwardly on strike, an attitude he doggedly maintained for a total of twelve years. His expensive school was wasted on him. He came away untamed and unmoulded as well as uneducated. Among Englishmen of his class – indeed, among Englishmen in general – it rendered him something of a lifelong outsider. Despite his years at Harrow, he never became a genuine product of the English public school system: not a man of understatement and arrogant self-effacement, not a cricketer, not a polished 'English gentleman', but rather a character from Shakespeare's England, where public schools were still unknown. And, in spite of his zealous autodidactic endeavours in later years and his own vast achievements in the fields of literature and historiography, he always lacked a solid, conventional education.

His second great childhood trauma was that he never really got to know his father. He followed Lord Randolph's rise and fall with 'vehement partisanship', daily devoured the speeches of his famous father in *The Times*, and studied the many caricatures of him in *Punch* more avidly than any school textbook. *In fact to me,* he wrote later, *he seemed to own the key to everything or almost everything worth having. But if I ever began to show the slightest idea of comradeship, he was immediately offended; and when once I suggested that I might help his private secretary to write some of his letters, he froze me into stone.*

Churchill long treasured one of the very few intimate conversations he ever had with his father, but even that had been prefaced by a sharp reproof for startling Lord Randolph by firing a shotgun at a rabbit in the garden. Winston was then an 18-year-old officer cadet at Sandhurst, his father a mere shadow of his former self. Having reprimanded Winston and seen how distressed he was, Lord Randolph regretted his outburst and apologized. *He explained how old people were not always very considerate towards young people, that they were absorbed in their own affairs and might well speak roughly in sudden annoyance.* He cordially enquired how Winston was doing, asked him about his impending entry into the army, and said he had arranged a small shooting party for him. *Then at the end he said, 'Do remember things do not always go right with me. My every action is misjudged and every word distorted . . . So make some allowances.'* That was all, but to his son and admirer those words were such an unwonted source of happiness that he could recall them verbatim a generation later.

Another pleasant but more momentous conversation had taken place three years earlier, when Winston was 15, though he misunderstood what underlay it. One day during the school holidays Lord Randolph came into the nursery and spent some time watching him and his younger brother setting out their toy soldiers in preparation for a large-scale battle. (Winston possessed nearly 1,500 toy soldiers, and he still played with them in an enthusiastic and realistic manner.) Eventually, Lord Randolph asked if he would like to join the army. Delighted by his father's sympathetic and understanding attitude, Winston eagerly said yes. That determined the next phase of his career. Lord Randolph had resignedly come to the conclusion that his son was not bright enough for anything else. The army was his only remaining chance.

But Winston Churchill had trouble getting into the army. Having twice failed the entrance examination for Sandhurst, he passed on the third occasion with marks so low that they qualified him only for the cavalry. (Cavalry officers were allowed to be more obtuse than infantry officers because they had to be wealthier, horses being expensive.) Lord Randolph had already written to the colonel-in-chief of a famous infantry regiment asking him to find his son a place; he now had the embarrassment of withdrawing his request. Moreover, horses were indeed expensive and the Churchills were not wealthy. That is to say, they were rich by normal standards but poor by those of the rich, devoid of a family fortune and deeply in debt. Lord Randolph wrote his son a stern paternal letter: if he didn't mend his ways he would end up a 'wash-out'.

Lord Randolph Churchill

Lord Randolph made a subsequent attempt to get Winston transferred to the infantry, but then lost interest. His life was nearing its end. His haggard face, hidden beneath a 'great beard', was that of a stranger, his mind had begun to wander. During his last conversation with Winston, Churchill's mother had to explain everything to him. He nodded, seemingly content, and asked in a distant but amiable way whether Winston now had his horses. On hearing that he did, he put out an emaciated hand and patted him on the knee. That last, vague gesture of friendship was another memory Winston would treasure for the rest of his life.

Young Churchill · 1895–1900

At 20 Winston Churchill was a hopeless academic failure who had not even gained his Higher School Certificate; an officer cadet at the third attempt; an embarrassment to his family; and, in his dying father's opinion, a potential 'wash-out'. In the ensuing five years, political circles in London spoke of him with steadily mounting interest, amusement, excitement, and – already, in some cases – expectancy. By 25, he was the talk of all England: he had become a national hero.

Those five years were the happiest time of his life. Much later, he wrote that the world had opened for him *like Aladdin's cave . . . Twenty to twenty-five! These are the years!*

He was now a professional soldier, a lieutenant in the hussars, and although peace reigned in Europe he managed, by dint of daring and initiative, to take part in five military campaigns: in Cuba, in India (twice), in the Sudan, and finally, with sensational and far-reaching results, in South Africa.

One finds this hard to credit. First an adolescence frittered away in forlorn unhappiness, and now this burning enthusiasm. It was as if an entirely different person had suddenly mounted the stage. Whence this transformation?

A key sentence occurs in Churchill's recollections of his early years: *I was now . . . the master of my fortunes.* All at once, nothing and no one was seeking to tame the untameable: no school, no cadet academy, no overpowering father. Lord Randolph Churchill's death spelled the end of a great, hopeless, rejected love. The profound and melancholy sense of liberation it engendered is one reason why, at the age of 21, young Winston Churchill shot forwards like a catapult suddenly released.

The other is that he at once, and almost by chance, discovered his innermost vocation: war.

No one will ever understand the phenomenon that was Churchill by regarding him simply as a politician and statesman who was ultimately destined, like Asquith or Lloyd George, Wilson or Roosevelt, to conduct a war. Nor was he a politician who had somehow to prove himself in war; he was a warrior who realized that politics forms part of the conduct of war. Compared to other British prime ministers of the twentieth century – Asquith, Lloyd George, Baldwin, Chamberlain, Attlee – he seems an alien from another world; but neither is he to be ranked among the professional soldiers of his time such as Foch or Ludendorff, Marshall or Montgomery, Zhukov or Manstein. To classify him correctly, we must think of other, older names: Gustavus Adolphus, Cromwell, Prince Eugene, Frederick the Great, Napoleon. They also include his ancestor the Duke of Marlborough, whose cast of mind he inherited.

All of these men were strategists, politicians, and diplomats combined, but it was only in and through war that they attained the pinnacle of their career. As Napoleon said of himself, they were 'born for war'. They instinctively understood it in all of its aspects: strategic, political, diplomatic, moral, and psychological. Moreover, in a way that a normal person finds hard to comprehend, they all loved the stark reality of war, the whiff of gunsmoke, the mortal danger, the lethal contest of man against man. It was in surveying and planning wars as a whole, with their constituent campaigns and battles, and perhaps in entering the fray themselves, that these brilliant practitioners of war found a self-fulfilment and happiness which (to them) surpassed all else. Churchill was a man of this type.

WARRIOR OR POLITICIAN

Churchill as a subaltern in the full dress uniform of the 4th Queen's Own Hussars at Aldershot in 1895

The young lieutenant of hussars may not have known this yet. It is probable that the strategic genius and daemon that dwelt within him, struggling and kicking to develop and assert itself, did not become fully apparent to him until 1914. What he did discover at once and with great delight, when he entered the anteroom of warfare by joining the army, was his affinity with war, his profound and innate understanding of it, and the fascination with the profession of arms that pervaded and enlivened his whole being. Previously he had been like a fish out of water. Now, all at once, he felt thoroughly at home and in his element. Boarding-school discipline he had loathed and wildly kicked against; military discipline, which was so much tougher, he positively adored. *There is a thrill and charm of its own in the glittering jingle of a cavalry squadron manoeuvring at the trot; and this deepens into joyous excitement when the same evolutions are performed at a gallop. The stir of the horses, the clank of their equipment, the thrill of motion, the tossing plumes, the sense of incorporation in a living machine, the suave dignity of the uniform – all combine to make cavalry drill a fine thing in itself.* He suddenly felt at home with his brother officers, too, although he was even less suited to them than to his schoolmates. As befitted cavalry officers, they were all rich, well-educated, and rather stupid, whereas Churchill was impecunious and ineducable, but an intellectual.

An intellectual! Now that the compulsion to learn had ceased, he was suddenly gripped by an urge to do so. He devoted long, hot days on garrison duty in India to reading like a man possessed – reading widely and indiscriminately: Plato and Darwin, Schopenhauer and Malthus, and, above all, Gibbon and Macaulay, the classical English historians who left their impress on his own style. He also began to write on his own account.

Apart from drilling, reading, writing, combing the map of the world for any minor wars that might be in progress, and wangling a place in the thick of them, he played polo. To officers in the crack British cavalry regiments of the day, polo was the *serious purpose of life*, and Lieutenant Churchill was a polo star. Even with a dislocated and bandaged arm he distinguished himself in the finals of the inter-regimental tournament and helped his regiment to win the coveted challenge cup. In short he was happy, and happiness released all his vital energy – of which, it now turned out, he possessed a double portion, no doubt inherited from his mother, the daughter of an American adventurer and great grand-daughter of a Native American.

That mother now entered his life. She had previously played a minor role compared to his idolized and unapproachable father, and she later receded into the background once more. She was not only an outstanding beauty – even in the 1890s, when she was in her forties – but an exceptionally vital woman who married twice more after Lord Randolph's death, the last time aged 68. But that lay in the future. During the years 1895–1900 she took an interest in the son who had suddenly developed such promise. She became his ally, gave him money, plotted with him, and exploited her numerous connections in London's high society on his behalf. *We worked together on even terms,* wrote Winston, *more like brother and sister than mother and son.*

And to what end did she exploit those connections? So as to ensure that Winston could be wherever 'something was going on' – in other words, wherever fighting was in progress. Winston had each time to be granted leave by his own regiment and attached to the relevant expeditionary force as a supernumerary officer, or aide, or war correspondent, or all three at once. The first time it was easy, the second time harder, and the fourth time was an adventure in itself, but mother and son always succeeded. On that fourth occasion – Kitchener's Sudan expedition of 1897, during which Lieutenant

The Sudan was under Anglo-Egyptian control in the late nineteenth century. Its Governor-General, General Charles Gordon, had instituted a religious and social reform campaign, which had alienated many native Muslims. The result was the rise of the Mahdi ('the divinely guided one'), Muhammad Ahmad, who led the reconquest of the region from the Egyptians and the British. Khartoum, the Sudanese 'capital', fell to Mahdist forces after a bitter siege in 1885. General Gordon was killed. But the Mahdi's victory was short-lived – he succumbed to typhus five months later.

Churchill participated in the last great cavalry charge in British military history at the Battle of Omdurman (1898) – the good offices of the Secretary of State for War and the Prime Minister had to be enlisted, because Kitchener was strongly opposed to the young man's presence. Churchill had already made himself unduly conspicuous, not only by forever thrusting himself to the fore, but even more so by voicing loud public criticisms after each of his military experiences.

By 1897, British interests in Egypt were increasingly threatened and a campaign was planned to reconquer the lands lost to the Mahdists. An Anglo-Egyptian force under General Kitchener routed the Sudanese at Omdurman (2 September 1898) and retook Khartoum.

For young Churchill had already, quite coincidentally, discovered his second profession during those five happy years. The first was war, the second literature.

What started it all was the need to finance his numerous military excursions abroad. Lord Randolph had died a poor man – his assets only just covered his debts – and his son was also on the poor side for a cavalry officer in an elite regiment. His mother gave him £500 a year, a tidy sum in those days, but it did not, of course, meet his requirements. Fortunately for

Horatio Herbert Kitchener (1st Earl Kitchener of Khartoum, 1850–1916), served as a soldier in Palestine and Cyprus before finding fame in the Sudan. As commander-in-chief of the Egyptian army from 1892, he led the Anglo-Egyptian reconquest of the Sudan, winning the battle of Omdurman (1898) and recapturing Khartoum. He later served as commander-in-chief in India and as Secretary of State for War in 1914. He was lost with HMS *Hampshire* off the Orkney Islands.

him, officers were not yet forbidden to act as war correspondents as well, so young Winston became a journalist. He began his first piece by stating that opening sentences were difficult – no less so in a newspaper article than in a declaration of love. His articles were reasonably successful, his fees slowly increased, and after his second campaign he decided to turn them into a book: *The*

Story of the Malakand Field Force (1898). Although well received in literary circles because of its vivid, graphic, and dramatic battlefield descriptions, it was less well received in military circles owing to the strictures Churchill directed at all and sundry: at the conduct of the campaign, the organization of supplies, and the whole army set-up, about which the self-assured young author found much to criticize. He had an exceptional faith in his own judgement, and pulled no punches. He also, in a rather ingenuous way, displayed a strategic sense and eye for generalship. Where he had acquired these, heaven alone knew, for he could produce no professional qualifications to legitimize them. Although this annoyed his senior officers, their superiors (the real leaders of London society) found it amusing, especially coming from the son of a famous and notorious father. In the military world, much as he loved it, Churchill was just a young subaltern; as a writer he gained influence and even tasted a *soupçon* of power.

So he continued to write. His next effort was a novel, which he later consigned to oblivion. His third book and first masterpiece, *The River War* (1899), was a broad account of British colonial developments and campaigns in Egypt and the Sudan, culminating in a description of his own experiences at Omdurman and criticizing General Kitchener for having desecrated the defeated Mahdi's tomb after the battle. In *The River War* Churchill for the first time instinctively devised a format of his very own – one that he later applied unchanged to his monumental descriptions of the two world wars: a blend of history and autobiography, analysis and eyewitness account. He enjoyed writing books almost as much as he relished the warlike adventures, perils, and triumphs they described; his love of words was as innate as his love of war: *It was great fun writing a book.*

Authorship had other advantages. It was relatively remunerative, whereas the life of a subaltern, especially one as extravagant as

Lieutenant Churchill, brought some rather alarming debts in its train. But writing also led to higher things. The youngster with the illustrious name and the mordant pen attracted the attention of powerful men. Government ministers invited him to their homes. Even the elderly and influential Conservative Prime Minister, Lord Salisbury, who had been almost continuously in office for 13 years, thought it worthwhile taking a look at him. As time went by, young Mr Churchill could not but notice what was expected of him: to go into politics and become a Member of Parliament – a Conservative MP, naturally; for a Churchill, anything else would have been unthinkable. Doors were opening; he had only to enter. Success, power, and fame awaited him, as did adventure, conflict, and danger. How could he hesitate? Politics was almost as exciting as war and just as dangerous, he once remarked to a fellow journalist. When the latter expressed mild scepticism, he added that in war you could be shot only once, in politics time and again. Spirited words, those; he had yet to learn how prophetic they were.

So young Mr Churchill had begun to discover his third, inescapable, all-embracing profession: politics. He was complete.

Churchill's political apprenticeship was less assured and more tentative than his military and literary beginnings, and he never became a true master of the political trade. He was not a born politician in the same way as he was a born warrior and writer. War and words came naturally to him, politics did not. They were imposed on him by his environment: in England politics were the only route to the very top, and that, most definitely, was the destination to which he aspired.

In 1899, sooner than foreseen, the Conservatives found him a constituency, though not a promising one: Oldham, a working-class town where a by-election had been called. Churchill did his best, but he lost as expected; his parliamentary career, which was to span over half a century, had got off to a false start. Though not a disaster, it annoyed him. For a short while in the summer of 1899, after four splendidly adventurous years of growing success, Churchill found himself rather at a loss. Having taken leave of the army that spring, he could not, for the moment, get into Parliament.

And then – he barely had time to worry about it – all his cares were banished by an extraordinary occurrence. It was like a bombshell, a grand transformation scene: his personal breakthrough.

In October 1899 the Boer War broke out in South Africa. Its only initial effect on Britain was a series of shocks and humiliations. The British Empire versus a couple of rebellious Boer republics?

The (second) Boer War (1899–1902) was the result of British attempts to gain political control over the Boer Republics (the Transvaal and the Orange Free State), and thereby over the gold mines of the Transvaal. In the first phase, Boer forces succeeded in humiliating the British in a number of engagements and besieged the towns of Ladysmith, Mafeking, and Kimberly. However, the British soon rallied and, under Kitchener and Earl Roberts, lifted the sieges and defeated the Boers in the field. In June 1900 Pretoria fell, but the war then entered a long and bitter phase during which the Boers used guerilla tactics to harry the British. At the Peace of Vereeniging (May 1902) British interests in South Africa were protected while the Boers maintained their control of native affairs.

Everyone expected it to be a military walkover. Instead, the first few months of the war brought several embarrassing defeats, and by November and December 1899 the disconcerted British were plunged in gloom.

When such a mood reigns – when everything goes unaccountably wrong and a nation begins to lose faith in itself – one brilliant feat of daring can assume disproportionate significance. In newspapers and in the public mind it can temporarily blot out any number of defeats in the same way as a hand held in front of the eyes can obscure an entire mountain range.

Such was the morale-booster administered by young Winston Churchill during that bleak late autumn of 1899.

The adventure he provided was not, in itself, so exceptional: he was taken prisoner, escaped his captors, and got clean away. A not unusual occurrence in wartime, but in this case it was the only ray of light in a dark night filled with dismal tidings – and besides, it made a wonderful story.

The story opened with a Boer attack on a British armoured train, a situation saved or at least half-saved by a courageous young man. He was (sensation!) only a war correspondent but had (second sensation!) taken command in the general confusion, uncoupled the locomotive, got all the wounded on board, and conveyed them to safety. While attempting to free the rest of the train he had then (sensation number three!) been taken prisoner. His name? (Sensation number four!) Winston Churchill, son of the famous Lord Randolph and author of some widely read and extremely controversial books of military criticism!

A few days later came the sad and terrible news that the Boers had shot young Mr Churchill. They might well have been within their rights to do so, since he had intervened in the skirmish as a

Churchill (*right*) a captive in Pretoria Prison 1899

ADVENTURES

journalist and civilian. He even had the gall to demand his release on those very grounds.

After a few weeks came glad tidings: Churchill was alive. Furthermore, he was at liberty. To top it all, he had pulled off a daredevil escape!

Thereafter – the story was not over yet – came all the exciting details of his adventure. How he had scrambled over a wall of the prison-camp in the midst of the enemy capital; how, without a map or a word of Afrikaans, he had tramped across the veldt with nothing in his pocket but a few bars of chocolate; how he had jumped aboard moving freight trains; how he had hidden in a mine and disclosed his identity to an English engineer there (who came from Oldham, his constituency!); and how he had eventually made his way by train to neutral Mozambique, concealed under some bales of wool.

How could this have failed to rejoice every heart, especially when the only other news items told of constant setbacks and disappointments? Churchill was now the hero of the hour, and he naturally behaved as heroes are expected to behave: he promptly reapplied for an officer's commission and spent the next six months participating in the campaign, which was gradually taking a turn for the better. At the same time he continued to write his vivid, graphic, lucid war reports, which explained why everything had gone so badly at first. Far from mincing his words, he inveighed against senile generals and bureaucratic muddles at the war ministry. He also knew how to do things better. Oh yes, young Mr Churchill knew a thing or two about war! When Pretoria was captured in July 1900 he accompanied the leading patrol that rode boldly into the city (which had yet to fall) and liberated the British prisoners of war housed in the camp from which he himself had escaped – a dazzling achievement. He continued to be the talk of the whole country.

In October 1900 – the Boer War seemed to be won and the Government was anxious to exploit the mood of victory – another general election was called. Churchill again took leave of the army. Wrapped in his new-found fame, he stood for Oldham once more, this time with success. He had made it. He had achieved his breakthrough. He was the most interesting man in the new Parliament, and had set his foot on the ladder at last. That winter he lived in a daze of self-confidence, a feeling that he was one of the elect, and he fascinated all who met him. A little while later, a fellow journalist with whom Churchill had sailed from South Africa to England wrote an enthusiastic profile of him entitled 'The Youngest Man in Europe'. Not just in England, in Europe! And, when Churchill undertook his first American lecture tour that winter (he still needed the money), an elderly Mark Twain introduced him to a New York audience as follows: 'Ladies and gentlemen, I have the honour to introduce Winston Churchill: hero of five wars, author of six books, and future Prime Minister of England.' He was half-joking, but only half; he was also half-serious, and young Churchill may secretly have shared such sentiments to the full.

This state of mind, which endured for a long time to come, may account for a strange lacuna in his life: no love affair occurs in his eventful, adventurous early years. We need not assume that the glamorous lieutenant of hussars, or later the youthful politician and man of the world, led a monastic existence. Indeed, his early recollections contain a few discreetly humorous allusions to the fact that he was no stranger to the ladies who frequented the promenade of London's Empire Theatre. But of a genuine love affair, a deeply felt relationship with a particular woman, we know nothing; and if such a love affair had existed we should doubtless know of it. London being a city addicted to tittle-tattle, few lives were so often and so thoroughly scrutinized and gossiped about as young Winston Churchill's.

He married late, when he was nearly 34. His marriage to Clementine Hozier, which laid the foundations of a lifelong and exemplary union, has sometimes been described as a love match. It was certainly no mere marriage of convenience or financial transaction: the bride had looks and breeding, but no money. The basis of the marriage was undoubtedly warm and genuine affection, and the sentence with which Churchill concludes *My Early Life* (1930) – *I married and lived happily ever afterwards* – is only one of many compliments he paid his wife in the decades to follow. For all that, one balks at the expression 'love match' and searches for a somewhat calmer, milder, more prosaic word than 'love'. One has only to remember the story of his parents' whirlwind engagement and marriage to detect the difference. There is a complete absence of the dramatic, romantic, sensational features so characteristic of Churchill's life in other respects. It was all so unruffled, so unadventurous and decorous. Their happiness was serene rather than 'stringent', and it is on record that the bridegroom eagerly absented himself during the wedding festivities for a political discussion with his ministerial colleagues.

Winston and Clementine Churchill at Hendon Airfield 1914

No, we shall have to accept that no great love affair or grand passion occurred in the adventurous existence of this passionate man. Churchill's life contained no Katharina Orlow, who almost sent Bismarck off the rails, nor an Inessa Armand, who did the same for Lenin. What really sent Churchill off the rails – more than once – were political passions and military ventures, never erotic ones. Churchill the politician was far from cold and calculating. He was warm-hearted and hot-blooded to an exceptional degree, perhaps for the very reason that all the warmth and ardour, all the passion and even the tenderness which other men expend in their private lives remained pent up in his public persona, undissipated and undiminished, and infused his public activities.

There are many great men whose lives might properly be divided into chapters bearing the names of various women. In contrast, the phases of Churchill's life should bear the names of the great offices to which he devoted himself: President of the Board of Trade; Home Secretary; First Lord of the Admiralty (a great, wonderful, tragic episode); Minister of Munitions; Secretary of State for War; Secretary of State for the Colonies; Chancellor of the Exchequer (a rather strange interlude in middle age); First Lord of the Admiralty once more (another turning point in his life); and then the belated culmination of his career as helmsman of the ship of state during the Second World War. These were Churchill's love affairs. This was where he fulfilled all the imagination and passion that was in him, each time in a different way, and this was where he found his heaven and his hell.

The Radical · 1901–1914

In a country governed by Parliament, a politician's home is his party. He not only subsists but must prevail and prove himself within it. It sustains and protects him. Without it he is nothing – a mere reed to be snapped by any passing storm. To a politician, especially in a country like Britain, where two well-established parties confront each other like hostile camps, changing parties is tantamount to emigration – or rather, to desertion in the face of the enemy.

Anyone who adopts such a course saddles himself with an almost insupportable political handicap: his old party regards him as a traitor, his new one as a suspect outsider. Churchill is the only known example in British parliamentary history of someone who did this and survived unscathed. He did it twice and survived both times – not unscathed, certainly, but triumphant.

Changing parties, even if only once, generally spells the end of a political career. In Churchill's case it was to be the beginning. It was, in a sense, his first act on becoming a politician. In March 1901 he delivered his maiden speech in the House of Commons as a newly fledged Conservative MP. On 31 May 1904 he crossed the floor of the House and took his seat on the Liberal benches.

The British political scene experienced a sensation reminiscent of one that had occurred 18 years earlier, when Lord Randolph Churchill threw away his office and career. The son's gesture was so like his father's: the same lordly, reckless nonchalance, the same incredible courage, arrogance, and exuberance, the same disregard for the hostility of hugely powerful men accustomed to obedience. The same apparent capriciousness and irrationality, too, for no one could believe that young Churchill had ever given any serious thought to the question of free trade versus protective tariffs, which was his pretext for changing parties. Nor is there any reason to believe this even now, given that Churchill displayed a cavalier indifference to economic problems throughout his life.

So what was his motive? The deserted and affronted Conservatives saw it as opportunism and ambition – unbridled, unprincipled, ruthless personal ambition. This explanation cannot be dismissed out of hand. However much the son's gesture resembled his father's, there was one obvious difference: Lord Randolph resigned when the Conservative Party (thanks mainly to his own efforts) had just come to power and could look forward to an indefinite period in Government, whereas Winston Churchill broke with his party when it was a spent force, worn out and disunited after 18 years in office, and a change of government was in the air. And there was another difference: Lord Randolph had thrown away his post as the government's second in command; when his son walked out on his party, he was a much talked-about but still very young and junior MP, an ordinary backbencher without a government post or status of any kind.

This may have been one reason for his reckless decision: Churchill was hurt and offended. He undoubtedly resented the fact that his party leaders had left him languishing on the backbenches for three long years. He yearned for office and power (less so for status); he craved it with every fibre of his being, and soon found it unbearable to lead the life of a backbencher who could do nothing but deliver speeches and file obediently past the tellers when the House divided.

Everyone who had dealings with Churchill in his early days in politics, or between 1901 and 1914, was struck by same thing: the pulsating restlessness and tense expectancy with which he metaphorically shuffled from foot to foot with impatience. This inner restlessness was composed of two elements: a firm belief that he was destined for great things, and an equally firm belief that he (like his father) would die young. The first assumption proved correct, as we all know; the second did not.

Churchill was not a religious man. He was never a Christian, and, like most agnostics, he was fatalistic – superstitious, if one will. He had often been in extreme danger in the course of his short life (indeed, he had repeatedly sought danger during his military adventures) and had always escaped it unscathed, sometimes in a truly miraculous fashion – an experience he would undergo on several future occasions. These he construed as unmistakable, repeatedly corroborated evidence that fate had something in store for him, and he was only too willing to let fate have its way.

He did not know, in these early years, what fate had preserved and marked him out for, but he held himself in constant readiness for the unknown signal. And, since he was just as firmly convinced at this time that he would die young, and was consequently in a hurry to fulfil his unknown destiny, it must naturally have driven him to despair to fritter away his years as a Conservative backbencher, pinned down by ageing political hacks who would at best have greeted his feverish sense of vocation with a pitying smile, and who now, to make matters worse, were clearly on the way out themselves.

Moreover, were they not the very same spiteful, narrow-minded men who had laid traps for his father, marred his career, and finally watched his political suicide with malevolent satisfaction? Wasn't the present Prime Minister the same Arthur Balfour who 20 years earlier had precociously advised Lord Salisbury to wait until 'Randolph' committed some flagrant breach of party discipline?

This was the period when Churchill wrote his father's biography (one of his great books), which appeared in two volumes in 1905. In so doing he relived the political dramas of the 1880s – relived them, so to speak, in the role of Lord Randolph Churchill. The latter had cherished a profound and insurmountable contempt for his parliamentary colleagues – a contempt of which it was hard to decide how much stemmed from an aristocrat's pre-democratic, baroque sense of nobility and how much from the impatient intellectual superiority of a brilliantly gifted man. His son shared that contempt to the full. From his seat on the Conservative back-benches at Westminster, Churchill saw himself surrounded by all the objects of his father's disdain: all the petty, tactical sagacity, prudence, calculation, and narrow-mindedness, all the mild arrogance and old-boy camaraderie of smug, wealthy, aristocratic mediocrities, successfully matured products of an expensive education based on flogging that had left its mark on them for life. And now, of all times, these imperturbable old gentlemen were obviously resigning themselves, with complacent, rather supercilious jocularity, to a few years (perhaps decades?) in opposition. They had temporarily reached the end of their tether, so let the Liberals govern for a while! What? What about those years, those fateful years in which something unprecedented might be waiting to be accomplished, perhaps the only years of life that still lay ahead for young Churchill (who was, after all, destined to die young)? Was he to spend them in idle, humble endeavour, pinned down on the opposition benches? No, thank you! Not him! He went over to the Liberals, where office, power, and possibly destiny awaited him.

He was a foreign body there, of course, but an interesting one, and, from the very first, a more important figure than he had ever been among the Conservatives. The Conservatives were a stolid, phlegmatically arrogant party impressed by nothing and no one, least of all by intellect and originality. They felt themselves to be the born rulers of the country, whereas their opponents, in those days the Liberals, still secretly felt that they needed something special in order to get into office for once: an exceptional slice of good luck, exceptionally good ideas, exceptional personalities. Thus a recruit as exceptional as the celebrated, notorious young Mr Churchill was extremely welcome to them. Almost from the first he was what he had never been with the Conservatives and might not have become for a long time: a ministerial candidate in a future Liberal government team. When the Liberals actually came to power after the famous landslide of January 1906, he was at once appointed Under-Secretary of State for the Colonies, a junior minister's post; two years later he joined the Cabinet, first as President of the Board of Trade and then as Home Secretary.

Thus far, everything was still relatively understandable. But now came a strange development, perhaps the strangest in Churchill's long political career. One would have thought that a former hussar officer and aristocrat who had defected to the Liberals would at least become something in the nature of his new party's right-winger. Instead, he sideslipped within a few years to its extreme left wing.

This 'radical' wing of the Liberal Party, which formed a kind of internal opposition to its upper-middle-class, moderate, highly educated leaders, was then being led with impassioned brilliance by a wild man and bugbear of the bourgeoisie, a poor, small-time solicitor from Wales: David Lloyd George. This sinister firebrand, born political genius, demagogue, incomparable rabble-rouser, and, when he chose, irresistible charmer, had a plan that struck terror not only into his Conservative opponents but also into many of his friends inside the party: he wanted to manoeuvre the Liberal government into a policy of social revolution that would permanently break the power of the Conservative ruling class (which he loathed), deprive it of its economic bedrock by imposing harsh inheritance and income taxes, neutralize its constitutional bastion,

David Lloyd George (1863–1945), Liberal MP for Caernarvon Boroughs from 1890, was Prime Minister from 1916 to 1922. Having served as Chancellor of the Exchequer, Minister of Munitions, and Secretary for War, he became premier after ousting the Liberal Herbert Asquith in alliance with the Conservatives. He was a dynamic politician and speaker, but his policies harmed the Liberal Party and hastened its decline.

the House of Lords, and enable the Liberals to win over the still largely disenfranchised proletariat by means of sweeping social reforms. During the years 1908 to 1911, politically the most turbulent in early twentieth-century Britain, he enforced that policy with guile and breathtaking political virtuosity, outplaying his own party leaders as well as the Conservatives. He lured them down paths of which they had never dreamed.

And who was his leading assistant and ally – almost his rival? None other than Winston Churchill the former Conservative. To the Conservatives this incredible development – even Liberal moderates shook their heads at it – seemed an unparalleled scandal. They looked on Lloyd George as an obvious enemy, but Winston Churchill? He was a Judas, a turncoat, a renegade, a class traitor who provoked hysterical loathing of a kind one would not readily expect from well-bred British Conservatives. When Churchill lost a by-election in 1908 (he quickly found himself another constituency and was re-elected to the House of Commons almost at once) the Tory *Daily Telegraph* announced with undisguised glee: 'Winston Churchill is out, Out, OUT!'

Churchill later found his way back into the Conservative Party. But never, not even in his greatest days, when the eyes of the whole world were upon him, did the Conservatives ever fully acknowledge him as one of their own.

But why this radical phase? He was certainly no born social revolutionary, rather the opposite; he was not even a genuine democrat by temperament or sentiment, more a romantic and baroque man with profoundly aristocratic instincts. True, those instincts also included, as they had in his father's case, a genuine sense of *noblesse oblige*, a well-nigh regal generosity, and a soft heart. There was also the fatalist who had suddenly perceived a summons from an unexpected quarter. Could that have been what fate had preserved him for, to become a great, aristocratic tribune of the people, a high-minded saviour of the poor? If so, he was ready.

An entry in the diary of Charles Masterman (later Churchill's Junior Minister at the Home Office) provides a clue. Churchill poured out all his hopes and ambitions to Masterman, who noted that Winston was 'full of the poor whom he has just discovered. He thinks he is called by providence to do something for them.'

That was one factor, but the other was that a genuine fight had broken out – and Churchill could never resist a fight. It was a class struggle – not what he had expected, not what he would have chosen, but a fight nonetheless. He could possibly have been on the other side; indeed, if he had thought it over calmly, that was where he belonged. But it was now too late for that, and there was no time for calm reflection. Now that he had taken sides and the fight was in progress, his natural instinct was to hurl himself into the fray, utterly, wholeheartedly, and with all his might.

There was also a third factor, this time of a personal nature: he was mysteriously, yet not so mysteriously, fascinated by and attracted to the really great tribune of the people with whom he was allying himself in this contest: Lloyd George. Outwardly, no two men could have been more different: Churchill the English aristocrat, Lloyd George the Welsh, Celtic member of the lower middle class; Churchill the pugnacious romantic versed in the politics of the day, Lloyd George the wily professional politician and realist; Churchill with his highly discreet and conventional private life, Lloyd George the notorious womanizer from whom no secretary was safe; Churchill the paragon of financial integrity (until an inheritance rendered him financially independent in 1919, he earned every penny he spent and often had money worries), Lloyd George, who was frankly corrupt, the only British politician of the century to amass a vast fortune during his term of office; Churchill almost suicidally courageous and in love with danger, Lloyd George physically rather timid and nervous; Churchill profoundly at odds with his own class, Lloyd George its hero and champion.

Yet the two men were bound together by something that distinguished them from all the other prominent ministers of the Liberal era: the well-educated, genteel, dignified, and almost wax-worklike figures who formed 'a cabinet of first violins', and who later, predictably enough, proved wanting in the First World War. The same applied even to Prime Minister Asquith, a man of excep-

tional authority, keen discernment, intellectual ability, and political expertise. He was arguably twentieth-century Britain's greatest peacetime Prime Minister, but he failed during the war, whereas Lloyd George, then an 'unwholesome' left-wing radical and almost a pacifist, pulled Britain together and led her to victory, just as Churchill would do in the Second World War. The pair were united

Herbert Henry Asquith (1852–1928), Liberal MP for East Fife, was Prime Minister from 1908 to 1916. After serving as Home Secretary (1892–5) and Chancellor of the Exchequer (1905–8), he became Liberal leader and Prime Minister in 1908. His administration oversaw the introduction of the old-age pension, payment for MPs, and reform of the House of Lords, but he was ill-suited to the demands of mass democracy and world war. He was replaced by Lloyd George in 1916.

PARTNERSHIP

by latent belligerence coupled with an artistic streak and a gambler's mentality: both pursued politics with a passion and an utter personal commitment that often appalled the normal, bourgeois politician. In short, both had genius and both were obsessives of a kind that struck the average, phlegmatic Briton as profoundly suspicious, but both possessed a demonic, elemental power that rendered them irresistible again and again, not only to the generality but – how could it be otherwise? – to each other as well.

It could not, at the same time, be disguised that they were also rivals. Both were boundlessly ambitious, and it was clear that one day there would not be room for both of them at the very top. For the moment, however, it was more a question of whether there would be room there for even one of them, or whether the massed ranks of the mediocre would bar their upward path for evermore. But for as long as this situation prevailed they were natural allies, brothers, and comrades-in-arms who vied with each other in their audacity and radicalism: 'terrible twins', as their opponents saw them.

Prime Minister Asquith had long been uneasy about this partnership, which often compelled him to go further than he really wanted. He also sensed that it embodied a force that might one day bring him down, so he eventually split it up. The way in which he did so was a tribute to his political and psychological acumen.

His method was quite simple: he deliberately appointed Churchill First Lord of the Admiralty at a time when war was looming on the horizon after the Agadir incident and the Moroccan crisis in the summer of 1911.

Having diagnosed the warrior that lurked within the radical, Asquith rightly concluded that he had only to set the warrior a task to be rid of the radical. Churchill's 'radical phase' was cast to the winds for good. The poor were forgotten. Fate obviously had a different and greater purpose in mind for him than 'doing something for them'. From the day he took over the Admiralty in October 1911, Churchill was waging war in spirit. As President of the Board of Trade, he had two years earlier backed Lloyd George, then Chancellor of the Exchequer, in denying the Royal Navy funds for new dreadnoughts at the height of its arms race with Germany. The 'twins' needed the

The so-called 'Second Moroccan Crisis' was sparked when a German gunboat, the *Panther*, appeared off the Moroccan port of Agadir in July 1911 to 'defend German interests' during the French-sponsored suppression of a local rebellion. International tensions were allayed when the Germans were compensated with territory in the Congo. Although a conflict was averted, the crisis proved to be a crucial step towards the First World War. The British drew closer to the French, and Germany became increasingly isolated.

money for their social reforms, and they also wanted to annoy the conservative-minded admirals. Now, year after year, Churchill submitted the most exorbitant navy estimates in British financial history. His partnership with Lloyd George was at an end.

Asquith had calculated correctly in another sense. The Royal Navy of 1911 was the largest ever, but by no means the most up-to-date. Not having had to fight a naval war for roughly a century, it was antiquated and proud and hidebound. It needed a man who could breathe new life into it. Asquith had originally thought of Lord Haldane (1856–1928), who had just reformed the British Army, but he knew what he was doing when he finally plumped for the much younger Churchill.

Churchill was still an inexperienced, rather weird, rather unpredictable politician, but he had from the outset proved to be an extremely reliable, dynamic, and versatile departmental minister. Fundamentally, administration suited him far better than politics, and Asquith had astutely recognized this. Young Churchill was much more of a born leader than a genuine politician: leading and giving orders, controlling and ruling were far more in his line than manoeuvring, scheming, and plotting. And as a minister he could rule – a circumscribed domain, admittedly, but rule it he could. Asquith perceived this and shrewdly exploited it.

Barely 37 years old, Churchill was more in his element than ever before. He now ruled the largest fleet in the world – ruled it almost absolutely and without any interference. He reorganized it, created a naval staff, revamped all its war plans, converted the entire fleet from coal-burning vessels to oil-burning, commissioned the construction of bigger ship's guns than had ever been built before and of entirely new types of ships to accommodate them – and all this without provoking or annoying his admirals and captains. On the contrary, Churchill made himself extremely popular with them, toured naval base after naval base and ship after ship, drank with officers in their cabins and listened to their complaints, concerns, and suggestions. He contrived to make them all feel that he was their man, and that he was at last fulfilling their long and vainly cherished aspirations.

Years earlier, Admiral Sir John Fisher had endeavoured to reform and modernize the British fleet in a way that had aroused the hostility of all the other senior officers in the Royal Navy. Now Lord Fisher and aged over 70, he was recalled from retirement by Churchill and secretly appointed as his personal think tank. This eccentric and embittered individual, a brilliant but half-demented old salt whose brain still teemed with the unfulfilled ideas he cherished like unborn children, watched with shining eyes as young Churchill, seemingly armed with a magician's wand, accomplished what he himself had broken his teeth on for years. He wrote Churchill veritable love letters beginning 'Beloved Winston' and ending 'Yours till hell freezes.' Churchill, for his part, looked up to the old man with admiration and often felt tempted, despite Lord Fisher's age and quirky temperament, to make him his First Sea Lord.

Regretfully, he kept postponing the appointment – Fisher was too much of an oddball, too difficult to deal with, too unpopular with his fellow officers – but he eventually, to his cost, made it.

In all he did at the Admiralty, Churchill focused his gaze on the major war with Germany and the German navy of whose inevitability he had been firmly convinced ever since the Agadir crisis of 1911.

Kaiser Wilhelm II

Affixed to the wall behind his desk at the Admiralty was a huge map of the North Sea on which the location of every German ship had to be daily marked with pins, and his first act on entering the office each morning was to check the current situation. War might break out any hour of any day, possibly triggered by a surprise naval attack like the Russo-Japanese War of 1904, and he, at least, was determined not to be caught napping.

Churchill had nothing against Germany and the Germans as such. He had happily attended the Kaiser's manoeuvres and was professionally admiring of the old German army and the young German navy. Even when he casually observed that a fleet was 'a kind of luxury' for Germany but a vital necessity for Britain – a statement much resented in Germany – he was not being deliberately unpleasant, merely telling the plain truth. But none of this altered the fact that he had since

German Emperor and King of Prussia from 1888 to 1918, Wilhelm II (1859–1941) was the eldest son of Frederick II and a grandson of the British Queen Victoria. From 1890 he ruled in person, displaying increasing instability and bellicosity, which inevitably contributed to international tensions and to the coming of the First World War. After abdicating in 1918, he lived in exile in the Netherlands until his death.

GERMANY

1911 considered a war with Germany unavoidable, rehearsed it in his mind every day, and was greatly fascinated by the prospect. He was a fighting man, after all. He found the thought of war intellectually bracing and inspiring, a spur to supreme, pleasurable exertion. His 'ambition' or faith in destiny, too, made his nerves tingle with delight at the thought of a future war he felt more able to cope with and conduct than anyone anywhere. He now believed he knew what fate had marked him out for.

On the night of his appointment as First Lord of the Admiralty in September 1911, he superstitiously opened the Bible that lay on his bedside table in the Prime Minister's country residence. What met his eye was the following passage:

'Hear, O Israel: Thou art to pass over Jordan this day, to go in to possess nations greater and mightier than thyself, cities great and fenced up to heaven,

'A people great and tall, the children of the Anakims, whom thou knowest, and of whom thou hast heard say, Who can stand before the children of Anak!

'Understand therefore this day, that the Lord thy God is he which goeth over before thee; as a consuming fire he shall destroy them, and he shall bring them down before thy face: so shalt thou drive them out, and destroy them quickly, as the Lord hath said unto thee.'

Churchill was no strict believer in the Bible, but he did have faith in that oracular pronouncement.

When war broke out just under three years later, it came as no surprise to him. On Sunday, 1 August, two friends dropped in for a hand of bridge. The cards had just been dealt when a big dispatch box was brought in to the room from the Foreign Office. Churchill took out his secret key from his pocket and removed a single sheet of paper. It read simply: 'War declared by Germany on Russia.'

According to Asquith, Churchill immediately 'got on all his war paint' and was 'longing for a sea-fight'. Lloyd George later described the scene in the Cabinet room as the British ultimatum expired at 11pm on 4 August 1914:

'Winston dashed into the room radiant, his face bright, his manner keen, and he told us, one word pouring out on the other, how he was going to send telegrams to the Mediterranean, the North Sea and God knows where. You could see he was a really happy man.'

The High-Flyer Crashes · 1914–1917

John Morley (1838–1923) was one of the wise old men of the Liberal Party. When people assessed the prospects of the two great political up-and-comers, he said that in peacetime he would put his money on Lloyd George, but that, if there were a war, Churchill would make mincemeat of him. Everyone fundamentally shared this opinion including Churchill and perhaps even Lloyd George himself. Churchill was patently born for war; Lloyd George was regarded almost as a pacifist.

Things turned out quite differently. Lloyd George became 'the man who won the war'. All eyes were on Churchill for a few months in 1914 and early 1915, but his high-altitude flight was brief and ended in a sudden crash. By May 1915 he was, politically, a ruined man.

Yet he started with a hand full of trumps. Only 39 when the First World War broke out, he was supremely self-confident and at the height of his physical and mental powers. As head of the British Admiralty he controlled one of the two most powerful instruments of war in the contemporary world (the other being the German army) and was one of the three men who determined Britain's conduct of the war during its first year (the other two being Prime Minister Asquith and Secretary of State for War Kitchener). He was also the only one of the three who possessed profound strategic discernment, a clear-cut concept, and creative ideas. This became his – partly self-induced – undoing, because it blinded him to the weaknesses of his political position.

Those weaknesses were plain to see. He was not a prime minister with unlimited powers, as he became in the Second World War. He was a Liberal minister in a Liberal cabinet whose parliamentary position was none too secure. The Conservatives thoroughly detested him; if a coalition government became necessary – and this possibility had to be allowed for in wartime – they would undoubtedly demand the scalp of this traitor to their party. Churchill had little firm support even among the Liberals and was still, basically, a 'sitter-in'. Public opinion, too, was gradually becoming a trifle uneasy about him. What with his change of parties, his exaggerated radicalism, and the new transformation that had overtaken him now that he headed the Admiralty and had suddenly developed an exclusive interest in ships, armaments, and war, nobody knew where they were with him. He had also made too many headlines over the years: as Home Secretary by employing London policemen to suppress rioting strikers in Wales, or by mounting and personally waging a veritable street battle against a handful of anarchists who had barricaded themselves inside a building in London's East End; as head of the Admiralty by sending warships to Ireland during one of the recurrent Irish crises and thus provoking a mutiny. He was forever creating sensations, perhaps involuntarily. It was his destiny – a kind of characteristic of his, and so much the worse for him. On the first occasion, in the Boer War, that characteristic had brought about his breakthrough, but it had harmed his reputation ever since. For all his acknowledged talent and brilliance, there seemed something unreliable and untrustworthy about him.

Churchill had no real backers. He did not get on with Lord Kitchener, the 'Sirdar' of the Sudan campaign of 1897, whom he had thoroughly annoyed as a pushy, vociferous young lieutenant. Kitchener was universally trusted and forgiven for all his failures. Churchill, in contrast, was regarded as untried and undependable.

He needed successes in order to hold his ground, even with Prime Minister Asquith, the ultimate authority, who initially let him have his head with a kind of sceptical, amused benevolence – not unappreciative of his talent and originality and not without hope, but also coolly prepared to drop him at any time.

Such was the position from which Churchill set out to direct the First World War. He took no trouble to secure or reinforce that position, and he upset his closest colleagues and assistants by constantly haranguing and barely listening to them. In their opinion, he behaved as if he knew it all. They were not so wide of the mark: he did indeed behave like that, but the tragicomic fact was, he really did know it all. In 1914 he was the only man in Britain who saw the military situation as a whole, and the only one with clear-cut ideas on how to win the war. Admittedly, he was obsessed with these ideas. He talked as if they must be as obvious to everyone as they were to himself, and he acted as if it rested with him alone to put them into effect.

Back in the summer of 1911, during the Agadir crisis, he had circulated to the Committee of Imperial Defence a memorandum on 'Military Aspects of the Continental Problem' which anticipated the events of August and September 1914 with uncanny prescience. He postulated it as certain that the Germans would march through Belgium and scythe southwards, in other words, operate in accordance with the Schlieffen Plan – of which he knew nothing, and which he replicated, so to speak, independently of Schlieffen. He correctly foresaw that the attacking German armies would compel

In 1905, German Field Marshal and Chief of Staff Alfred von Schlieffen (1833–1913) devised a plan for conflict with the French and Russians. He anticipated a swift victory in the west against France before throwing the bulk of Germany's forces against the Russians in the east for a longer campaign. In the event, the Schlieffen Plan failed. The French were not defeated and Germany was forced to fight a protracted war on two fronts; exactly what Schlieffen had sought to avoid.

THE SCHLIEFFEN PLAN

the French to withdraw from the Meuse Line some 20 days after mobilization, and that they would, after some 40 days, be *extended at full strain* and ripe for a counterattack *if the French army has not been squandered by precipitate or desperate action*. In fact, the first Battle of the Marne culminated in a German retreat on 10 September 1914, precisely 40 days after mobilization.

Churchill also foresaw, with the same visionary clarity, what had suddenly become the strategically decisive point: Antwerp.

The fact was that both huge armies had one flank exposed after the Battle of the Marne: the Germans on the right, the Allies on the left. The inevitable consequence was what later became known as 'the race to the sea', namely, an attempt by each side to outflank the other in the only possible direction. The isolated Belgian fortress of Antwerp was still holding out in the north. If it could be reinforced and relieved in time from Britain, and if all available British reserves were sent across the Channel to the new Antwerp front, it should be possible, using Antwerp as a base, to bar German access to the Channel coast, prevent the front line from congealing, catch the Germans' right wing as it moved northwards, and roll it up.

The Germans, who clearly saw this, concentrated all their reserves on eliminating Antwerp as quickly as possible after the Battle of the Marne. No one in Britain saw it except Churchill, and Churchill's insight was not matched by the extent of his authority.

He now did something that was not only bold but proved the first step on the road to his subsequent downfall. He betook himself to Antwerp to attend to matters in person, assumed command there without due authorization, and hinted at the imminent arrival of large British reinforcements. More than that, he sent the Prime Minister a telegram asking to be released from his post as First Lord of the Admiralty, reactivated (he had, after all, been an army officer), and placed in command of the Antwerp front. He also requested more troops and – still in his capacity as head of the

Admiralty – ordered two naval brigades to Antwerp. The only ground forces at his disposal, these consisted largely of recruits still in training, and most of them were eventually taken prisoner. In short, he endeavoured by means of extreme personal involvement to coerce his cabinet colleagues into a strategic improvisation whose purpose was clear to him but not to them. It was bound to end in disaster.

Churchill's Antwerp venture was not entirely fruitless, however. It prolonged the fortress's wavering resistance by five days, gaining just enough time for the ponderous Allied armies to end 'the race to the sea' in a dead heat with the Germans. But that had not been Churchill's idea. No one had grasped – nor had he succeeded in explaining – his plan to reinforce Antwerp swiftly and substantially, turning it into the base for a counterattack on the rear of the German armies pushing northwards and winning the war in the west before it could congeal into static trench warfare. All that remained was universal head-shaking at his eccentric behaviour and raised eyebrows at the ruthless sacrifice of his naval recruits. To the public, and to his colleagues, he seemed a man prepared to throw away one of the highest offices of state on a sudden whim, for the sake of a local military adventure which had then, on top of everything else, gone wrong! He had taken a bad knock.

But he was not disheartened even now, and his strategic discernment was unimpaired. Once the Western Front had become bogged down in the trenches, he clearly saw that there were only two remaining routes to victory: either something must be devised that would defeat the trenches, a 'land ship' that would run over them and bury everyone inside; or the Allies should perform a gigantic outflanking movement from the Balkans in South-East Europe – one that would open up a new front devoid of trenches and strong defences.

In the winter of 1914–15 Churchill set about taking both routes –

once again on his own initiative. It is noteworthy that the Allies achieved their victory in 1918 by those two very means: the tank, the end product of Churchill's 'land ship' experiments, finally lent their hitherto fruitless offensives on the Western Front tactical superiority over the German defences; and the collapse of Turkey and Bulgaria, which breached Germany's open and undefended southeast flank, prompted General Ludendorff to throw in the towel on 29 September 1918. But Churchill derived scant benefit from this belated vindication of the proposals he had advanced in 1914. Initially regarded as a fanciful whim and dismissed by the army because it stemmed from the Admiralty, Churchill's 'land ship' or 'tank' idea remained entangled for years in a thicket of conservative, bureaucratic objections. The Balkan Front idea did not: Churchill pushed it through, all opposition and misgivings notwithstanding, but only in an attenuated form. Its final outcome was the ill-starred Dardanelles or Gallipoli campaign, which brought him down.

His strategic concept was grandiose. Turkey, allied with Germany since October 1914, was relatively weak. The maritime location of her capital, Constantinople, rendered it vulnerable to attack by superior naval forces. If Constantinople fell, Turkey herself would probably collapse. This would at least establish a secure sea route to Russia, whose already depleted offensive strength could be restored by means of massive arms shipments. In addition, however, Serbia was still holding out, Bulgaria had yet to ally herself with Germany, and powerful political forces in Greece and Romania were ready to side with the Allies if they won a victory in the region. The fall of Constantinople would provide the awaited signal, and the Balkans would burst into flames like a forest fire. From there, Austria could be brought to her knees, completely isolating Germany and threatening her with a war on three fronts instead of two! This was strategy on a Napoleonic scale. It was also made to measure for Britain, with her vast naval forces and small

THE STRATEGIST

Dardanelles campaign, Gallipoli, Fort de Sedd El-Bahr

but efficient army – far more suitable than the slow recruitment and training of immense armies destined for insertion in the bone-mill operated by static battles on the Western Front.

Except that the implementation of such a scheme – and the Second World War made this still more obvious – necessitated amphibious warfare, or very close co-operation between the Navy and the military. This seemed unachievable: Lord Kitchener 'did not believe in the Dardanelles', he believed in the possibility of a breakthrough on the Western Front. Churchill's first mistake lay in being too proud to talk Kitchener round – as it later transpired that he might have done. Kitchener eventually, in a rather half-hearted way, volunteered to 'assist' the Navy if it failed to do the job alone. But Churchill had meantime resolved on a sudden vigorous attack with naval forces alone.

While not impossible, perhaps, this was an immensely audacious venture of the kind that can succeed only if all those undertaking it co-operate with faith and enthusiasm, excelling themselves in the process. Churchill's second mistake was to continue with his plans even though he had to almost drag his admirals along with him. They reluctantly, apprehensively allowed themselves to be persuaded. Churchill either overrode their reluctance or may possibly have failed to notice it altogether. The consequences were inevitable.

On 18 March 1915 the fleet had practically silenced the Turkish forts overlooking the Dardanelles – though not without considerable losses – after a massive artillery duel. If a naval *coup de main* was to be risked against Constantinople, it was now or never. But the admirals, perhaps rightly, had become too chary of the undertaking, and, since Kitchener had meantime agreed to 'assist' the fleet, they decided to wait for the army instead. It was slow to arrive, however. On 25 April British troops landed on the Gallipoli peninsula and established a bridgehead there. They never broke out of that bridgehead: the element of surprise had been squandered. The Turks had concentrated in full strength and held their ground. By the middle of May it was clear that Churchill's grand, war-winning scheme had accomplished no more than the creation of another static front in far-off Turkey.

What now? Churchill was all for sticking it out. For the first time, he displayed the bulldog-like obstinacy that had hitherto lain hidden beneath his love of adventure and bold improvisation. He was prepared to double the stakes, throw in the most modern, powerful warships, and carry out a second landing in the Turkish rear. Stubbornly, he advocated a strategy of *Now's the time!*

But the admirals vetoed this, foremost among them his old, tough, much admired friend Lord Fisher, whom he had six months earlier recalled to the Admiralty in the face of many objections and warnings. All had gone well between them for a few months – indeed, Fisher had initially endorsed Churchill's Dardanelles plans – but he was one of the first to detect a fly in the ointment. Although Churchill, for whom Lord Fisher cherished his own brand of affection, had talked him round a few times, he subsequently regretted his weakness and became an even tougher and more resolute opponent. The Dardanelles were Churchill's baby, not his. Lord Fisher's baby was the fleet, whose finest units Churchill now proposed to place in jeopardy. Whether or not Churchill's Dardanelles plan had originally been a good one, it had now become a thoroughly botched undertaking. There was only one answer: End it! Write it off! Escape from the trap! Save the fleet!

Relations between the young head of the Admiralty and his old First Sea Lord during May 1915 were superheated and dramatic.

Admiral Lord John Fisher. Churchill's devotion to Fisher, King of the Dreadnoughts, would result in his fall from office following the failure of the Dardanelles Campaign

CHURCHILL AND LORD FISHER

The young man and the old, both dogged fighters by nature, both proud, headstrong, and egocentric, both utterly convinced of the rightness of their cause, had a fondness and admiration – indeed, a love – for each other. Neither was willing to surrender his power over the other; each wanted to continue the close collaboration which they themselves had jokingly referred to, only a few months earlier, as 'our happy marriage'; and both wanted to reimpose their former mutual trust, but on terms that were mutually quite unacceptable and intolerable. Churchill, in particular, wooed the old man with steadfast, unyielding charm and thought he had won him back each time. He failed to realize that it was Lord Fisher's temporary weakness that rendered him all the more bitter, filling him with bile and a thirst for revenge. By Saturday, 15 May, Lord Fisher had had enough. He tendered his resignation in language that verged on the offensive: 'I am unable to remain any longer as your colleague.' Then he quit the Admiralty without saying good-bye and remained incommunicado thereafter. He also promptly informed the Conservative Party leaders of his resignation, well knowing that he would provoke a government crisis and bring about Churchill's downfall. Characteristically, Churchill failed to see this. He was so busy waging war, he had ceased to take any notice of the political developments at home on which his ability to wage war was wholly dependent.

The position of Asquith's Liberal government had been rapidly deteriorating in the spring of 1915. War on the Western Front had brought its disappointments, the Dardanelles expedition was clearly making no headway, and the Press had exposed grave defects in the supply of munitions. The renowned Lord Fisher's dramatic resignation was the last straw. The Conservatives issued an ultimatum: either a coalition, or a parliamentary vote of no confidence. Realizing that a parliamentary debate at this juncture would inevitably end in disaster for the Government, Asquith – and Lloyd

George – decided on a coalition. But this meant, among other things, that Churchill had to be sacrificed. The Conservatives, as everyone knew, regarded him as insupportable.

Lord Fisher had resigned on Saturday. Churchill spent Sunday putting together a new Board of the Admiralty, but on Monday, when he went to see Asquith with his list of new appointments, the Prime Minister told him it was too late. A far more radical step had become necessary, namely, a government reshuffle. 'What are we to do with you?'

Churchill never forgot that 17 May 1915. It was a day on which his personal god, destiny, played cat and mouse with him. Asquith's 'What are we to do with you?' brought Churchill his first dire warning that he was in danger – and, at the same time, the lightning realization that he was done for. It came as a terrible shock. He was still struggling to regain his composure when there was a knock at the door: a message from the Admiralty summoning him back at once. The German fleet was about to put to sea.

Churchill spent the evening and night of that day with his admirals at the chart table, supervising the British fleet. As the Morse signals came and went, he saw himself alternately as a discarded minister and victor of the greatest naval engagement in history. All was still in the balance, and he retained his faith in destiny.

By morning it was all over: the German fleet had turned away and the great naval battle was deferred – for almost exactly a year, as it turned out. Churchill had fallen. His successor at the Admiralty was Arthur Balfour, the former Conservative Prime Minister who had spurned him eleven years earlier. Churchill was appointed to the Chancellorship of the Duchy of Lancaster, an unimportant sinecure, and even that Asquith had wangled out of the Conservatives only because it enabled Churchill to join the newly formed, eleven-man 'Dardanelles Committee', where he would, so to speak, be on trial. He was bereft of executive authority and had little influence. His loyal and admiring supporter Violet Asquith, who tried to console him, found him a broken man. He did not even have a bad word to say about his disloyal but admired friend Lord Fisher, who had brought him down. *No – I'm done,* he kept saying. *No – I'm finished.*

That summer was a terrible time. Churchill later wrote that he had felt like a deep-sea fish abruptly brought to the surface, with the result that its head threatened to burst. He had grown accustomed to the constant pressure of immense strains, decisions, and responsibilities; suddenly deprived of this pressure, he realized that he had forgotten how to live without it. Membership of the Dardanelles Committee made matters even worse. As he himself put it, he knew everything but could no longer do anything.

Churchill preserved his sanity that summer by starting to paint. Hitherto undiscovered by himself, his considerable artistic talent became a comfort to him, a kind of drug or medicine which he never abandoned thereafter. Meanwhile, however, the war dragged on. Was he to spend it as an amateur painter? As his mental energies slowly returned, a fantastic new plan took shape in his mind.

He realized that he had failed as a politician and a minister. As long as the coalition remained in power – probably for the duration of the war – a comeback was unthinkable because the Conservatives hated him too much. But hadn't he been an army officer as well, and couldn't an officer scale the heights in wartime? Perhaps his great mistake had been to try to play Napoleon as a parliamentary minister; Napoleon had been an army officer.

True, Churchill had left the army as a humble lieutenant, but he had since been head of the Admiralty, and many ranks could be leapfrogged in wartime. Even Kitchener, who did not like him, had not objected at the time of Antwerp to summarily appointing him a major-general if he were set on the idea. Nothing had come of this at the time, but why shouldn't what had been possible then be

　　　　　　　A FAILED POLITICIAN

possible now? Sir John French, the British commander-in-chief on the Western Front, was an old friend. He would at least entrust him with a brigade. That would be sufficient to enable him to distinguish himself by means of some brilliant solo operation. Then would come a division, a corps, an army, and some day – who could tell? – perhaps supreme command.

He had toyed with such ideas earlier on. Asquith noted shortly after Antwerp: 'I have had a long call from Winston, who, after dilating in great detail on the actual situation, became suddenly very confidential and implored me not to take a conventional view of his future. Having, as he says, tasted blood these last few days, he is beginning, like a tiger, to raven for more, and begs that sooner or later – and the sooner the better – he may be relieved of his present office and put in some kind of military command. I told him that he could not be spared from the Admiralty, but he scoffs at that, alleging that the naval part of the business is practically over, as our superiority will grow greater and greater every month. His mouth waters at the sight and thought of Kitchener's new armies. Are these "glittering commands" to be entrusted to "dug-out trash" bred on the obsolete tactics of 25 years ago, "mediocrities who have led a sheltered life mouldering in military routine," etc., etc.? For about a quarter of an hour he poured forth a ceaseless cataract of invective and appeal, and I much regretted that there was no shorthand writer within hearing, as some of his unpremeditated phrases were quite priceless. He was, however, three parts serious and declared that a political career was nothing to him in comparison with military glory.'

That had been a year ago. Now he was in deadly earnest.

In November, when it had at last been decided to wind up the Dardanelles expedition, he took his leave of the Lower House with a grand, dignified gesture: he would now take up *other duties*. Three days later, reactivated with the rank of major, he was on his way to France.

It turned out to be a sadly unsuccessful venture. Sir John French had promised Churchill a brigade, but French himself was beginning to fall out of favour and could no longer get his way. The most the army was prepared to offer Churchill was a battalion and the rank of lieutenant-colonel. So he was now a common or garden front-line soldier whose privilege it was to conduct delousing campaigns in the trenches of muddy Flanders; any other form of operation exceeded his sphere of authority. Moreover, he was given a very frosty reception by the staunchly Conservative guards battalion to which he was initially assigned. Its officers had no time for turncoat politicians and class traitors, and they let him feel this.

Churchill was no worse a front-line officer than any other. He had never lacked courage, and he possessed a sense of humour. Danger did not frighten him, nor did the rigours of life in a muddy trench in winter. It was just that he could not, in the long run, blind himself to the futility and superfluity of the whole venture. What was he doing there? What was he achieving by submitting to the tedium of trench warfare routine like a thousand others? Honesty compelled him to admit that he was burying his talent.

He also underwent special humiliations that continually reminded him how wrong and inappropriate his situation was. Members of Parliament and diplomats touring the front line heard tell of the fallen celebrity who could be viewed, free of charge, in a British trench. They either came to inspect the miraculous beast or requested his presence. On one occasion this saved his life: he had just left his dug-out, bound for one such command performance, when it sustained a direct hit. (An omen like so many others? Was he being preserved for greater things? Perhaps destiny had not forgotten him after all.) Even so, it was hard to stand to attention in front of people with whom he had recently dealt on equal terms, often from a superior position. Not only hard but really quite unnecessary.

After six months, Churchill took advantage of some leave to deliver a parliamentary speech in which he aroused universal consternation by recommending his successor at the Admiralty to recall Lord Fisher. Another few months, and he once more bade farewell to the army (a step ungraciously sanctioned on condition that he did not reapply for a commission while the war lasted). He returned to London and resumed his seat in the House of Commons. It was not a glorious homecoming.

The war continued and time went by. The great naval engagement for which Churchill had spent three years eagerly preparing the British fleet took place and ended in a draw. He had nothing to do with it. Asquith's government fell and Lloyd George assumed the wartime premiership. There was no place in his government for Churchill: the Conservative Party leader, Andrew Bonar Law, was steadfastly opposed. The year 1917 saw Britain threatened with defeat by the U-boat blockade, America's entry into the war, the Russian Revolution, French mutinies, protracted fighting in Flanders. Churchill was a mere spectator of all these events. *I knew everything; I could no longer do anything.* And that was the way

Andrew Bonar Law (1858–1923), Conservative MP for Glasgow Blackfriars, was Prime Minister from 1922 to 1923. Entering Parliament in 1900 and becoming leader of the Conservative Party in 1911, he became Chancellor of the Exchequer in Lloyd George's coalition government in 1916. Fearing a split in his party, Bonar Law then led (albeit reluctantly) a Conservative revolt against the coalition in 1922, thus bringing about Lloyd George's downfall and his own elevation to Prime Minister.

it stayed. He solaced himself by painting landscapes and delivering the occasional speech in the House of Commons, but he suffered deeply. *I am simply existing,* he told Lord Fisher. He did not know what we know today: that this was not the end. Defeated and rejected, he felt like a prisoner under *sentence of continued and indefinite inactivity.*

The Reactionary · 1917–1929

It was his old friend and rival, Lloyd George, to whom Churchill owed his re-emergence from the abyss into which he had plunged.

This rescue operation was no easy task for Lloyd George either. He himself was playing for high stakes, a dangerous game that ended six years later in his own definitive downfall. By forcing his old chief Asquith out of office late in 1916 he had split his own Liberal Party and driven the bulk of it into opposition. In Asquith's coalition government the Liberals had still been the senior partner. Lloyd George's coalition was one quarter Liberal and three-quarters Conservative. Furthermore, he had until recently been a red rag to the Conservatives, so governing with their support for almost six years was a dazzling feat of political virtuosity. As for persuading the Conservatives to accept their former arch-enemy, Churchill the party traitor, that seemed a total impossibility. But this may have been the very reason why it attracted the 'Welsh wizard' – that and the fact that Lloyd George saw Churchill as a genuine personal reinforcement, a rare kindred spirit and the only other British politician with a spark of hellfire. Having Churchill at his side in a position of complete dependence – being able to use Churchill's wealth of imagination and energy as he pleased – that, to Lloyd George, seemed a worthwhile objective.

When he first formed a government in December 1916, it still proved impossible. The Conservative Party leader, Bonar Law, a tough and inflexible man, could not be bullied or persuaded. Lloyd

George was also reminded by Lord Curzon (1859–1925) that he had agreed to join the War Cabinet only on condition that Churchill be excluded. 'He is a potential danger in opposition,' wrote Lord Curzon. 'In the opinion of us all he will as a member of the Government be an active danger in our midst.' And so Lloyd George had, for the time being, to dispense with Churchill's services.

Six months later, in July 1917, Lloyd George appointed Churchill nonetheless, and without consulting anyone. Having rendered himself indispensable in the interim, he thought he could afford to do so. There was still an outcry – almost, for a day or two, a government crisis. *The Morning Post* summed up the mood: 'That dangerous and uncertain quantity, Mr Winston Churchill – a floating kidney in the body politic – is back again at Whitehall. We do not know in the least what he may be up to, but from past experience we venture to suggest that it will be everything but his own business.' As Lloyd George later wrote in his *War Memoirs*: 'Some of them [the Conservatives] were more excited about his appointment than about the war. It was a serious crisis. It was interesting to observe in a concentrated form every phase of the distrust and trepidation with which mediocrity views genius at close quarters. Unfortunately, genius always provides its critics with material for censure – it always has and always will. Churchill is certainly no exception to this rule.'

The following passage is one of the most perceptive ever written about Churchill, and says a great deal about its author. Lloyd George raises the question of why Churchill made so many sworn enemies and had no real supporters. Everyone conceded that he was 'a man of dazzling talents, that he possessed a forceful and a fascinating personality. They recognized his courage and that he was an indefatigable worker ... Some of the greatest figures in British political life had ended in a different party from that in which they commenced their political career. That was therefore not an adequate explanation of his position in public confidence. They asked: What then was the reason?

'Here was their explanation. His mind was a powerful machine, but there lay hidden in its material or its make-up some obscure defect which prevented it from always running true. They could not tell what it was. When the mechanism went wrong, its very power made the action disastrous, not only to himself but to the causes in which he was engaged and the men with whom he was co-operating. That was why the latter were nervous in his partnership. He had in their opinion revealed some tragic flaw in the metal. This was urged by Churchill's critics as a reason for not utilizing his great abilities at this juncture. They thought of him not as a contribution to the common stock of activities and ideas in the hour of danger, but as a further danger to be guarded against.

'I took a different view of his possibilities. I felt that his re-sourceful mind and his tireless energy would be invaluable under supervision.'

The fact is that during the eventful five years 1917–22, in which he once more played an important part, held high offices, and rendered great service to his country, Churchill was not really him-self, but more in the way of Lloyd George's shadow. He very soon became Lloyd George's closest and most valued assistant – but only his assistant; the final decision always rested with Lloyd George.

Years later, when the partnership was long dissolved, Churchill a Conservative minister once more, and Lloyd George an impo-tent, isolated member of the Opposition, there was a reconciliatory meeting: Lloyd George called on Churchill at the Treasury. It was a lengthy visit. When Lloyd George had gone, Churchill's private secretary (who later told the story) came in with the signature folder and found Churchill lost in thought in front of the fireplace. It was strange, he said, looking up. Before a quarter of an hour had elapsed they had re-established their former relationship. And then, with an odd expression that froze his young assistant's smile on his lips, he defined it as the relationship of master and servant.

These years were in many respects a brilliant and highly meritorious period in Churchill's life, but also the years in which he was least himself. He was 'under supervision' in the service of another man – one, moreover, whose light was bright enough to dim his own. Churchill was Minister of Munitions until the Armistice, then Secretary of State for War (1918–21) and Minister of Air (1919–21), then Secretary of State for the Colonies (1921–2). He proved his mettle in all these capacities, just as he had in his former posts. Churchill had always been an outstanding departmental minister, brimming with ideas and energy (though inclined to meddle in his colleagues' departments), and almost all of his spells in office are associated with some achievement of historical importance. As Minister of Munitions, for example, he was responsible for the mass production of tanks; as Secretary of State for War for the rapid and complete implementation of demobilization plans, which nipped a mass mutiny in the bud; and as Secretary of State for the Colonies for the pacification of the Middle East and a major share in the pacification of Ireland. All of this was hard and valuable work – expert work, but somehow impersonal. While zealously and vigorously helping, in Lloyd George's service, to straighten out the dislocated post-war world and administer it after a fashion, he was – perhaps without realizing it at first – becoming restive and resentful. When Lloyd George fell in October 1922, Churchill fell with him, but inwardly he had already severed relations with his boss. Lloyd George never made a comeback. Churchill, to everyone's astonishment, was back in office only two years later – as a Conservative minister.

It beggared belief: the party traitor and *bête noire* of every good Conservative had suddenly, after a mere two years, returned as a leading Conservative MP and senior cabinet minister – as Chancellor of the Exchequer, no less!

Churchill had pulled off an incredible, daredevil, seemingly impossible stunt – and one rendered no easier by the fact that he had been secretly flirting with it for years. Lloyd George had once issued him with a blunt warning: A rat could desert a sinking ship, but it couldn't climb back on board if the ship didn't sink after all.

This second change of party was not, of course, as easy as the first. He did not simply stroll with lordly nonchalance from one side of the House of Commons to the other. For two years, from the end of 1922 to the end of 1924, he had no parliamentary seat at all and failed to win three different seats in the three general elections held during that period.

He was somewhat assisted by the signs of dissolution manifest in the old, rigid two-party system. A new climate had prevailed since 1918 in British domestic politics as elsewhere. The Liberals were split and hopelessly debilitated, the Labour Party was emerging on the Left as the new party of the masses, and the Conservatives, too, were temporarily threatened with disintegration after the end of the coalition and the breach with Lloyd George. Some of their ablest people had grown used to coalition government and would have liked to perpetuate it.

Churchill went a step further: he advocated the formation of a new 'centre party' composed of Lloyd George Liberals and pro-coalition Conservatives. It is hard to tell whether he was really in earnest, or whether he wanted to alarm the Conservatives and exert a little pressure on them. At all events, their new leader, Stanley Baldwin, eventually decided – unlike his predecessor Bonar Law – that it would be the lesser of two evils to have this dynamic, dangerous, and indefatigable man on his side rather than against him. He took him back into the party and even, after the Conservative election victory in November 1924, gave him a senior but unsuitable ministerial post. This put paid to any more talk of the centre party project.

It is just understandable, under these circumstances, that the Conservatives should have taken Churchill back – though not without great reconciliation scenes, considerable reservations, and persistent covert hostility. But why was Churchill so doggedly determined to rejoin them?

That an element of opportunism was involved cannot be ignored or extenuated. The Conservatives were in the ascendant in 1924,

Stanley Baldwin

just as the Liberals had been in 1904, and Churchill, now as then, was eager not to be left out. His thirst for action was unassuaged, and he had a lifelong horror of wasting away in idle, impotent opposition. There was a kind of childishly innocent ruthlessness about his desire to exercise power, and he always privately felt, like a baroque politician, that he was thoroughly entitled to trim his sails to whichever wind happened to be blowing. Party loyalty and adherence to the abstract, ideological principles of the bourgeois parliamentarian were always alien to him. Anyone who wanted to better himself had to change, and anyone who strove for perfection had to change very often: such was his response to a critic who reproached him for his frequent changes of view and position.

Although Churchill meant this ironically – cynically, if one will – a genuine transformation had taken place in him. His second change of party was less purely opportunist than his first (though opportunist it was): the former radical had unmistakably become a reactionary. The event that had bowled him over and changed his mind was the Bolshevik Revolution in Russia.

Had Churchill ever been a genuine 'leftist', a bona fide radical? Lloyd George, who was one, and whose left-wing radicalism Churchill had seemingly emulated for a while, never believed so. He always regarded Churchill as a secret Tory, and it is probable that his keen eye did not deceive him. Churchill's radicalism was the magnanimous, youthful whim of a grand seigneur. He wanted to annoy the stupid, arrogant members of his class; he also, being as soft-hearted and broad-minded as he could be, had a genuine desire to do something for his new discovery, the poor – but only, of course, with the natural proviso that he remained a grand seigneur and that the poor, for whom he chivalrously fought, remained the poor. Genuine class struggle and upheaval, social revolution with all its gory horrors, the inversion of the lowest and highest, the ousting of the mighty from their seats of power – that had not been part of the bargain. When all these things actually happened in Russia, they blew away Churchill's radicalism like thistledown, and he reacted like some baroque prince confronted by a peasant insurrection. Lloyd George sarcastically observed that Churchill's 'ducal blood revolted at the wholesale slaughter of Grand Dukes'. Lloyd George himself, who had personally suffered from aristocratic arrogance in his youth, could view this extermination with far more serenity.

As Lloyd George's Secretary of State for War, Churchill used all his influence during the Russian civil war of 1919, and again during the Russo-Polish War of 1919–20, to escalate British

The process by which Lenin's Bolsheviks came to power in Russia began with the abdication of the Tsar in February 1917 following widespread demonstrations against the prosecution of the war. There then ensued an eight-month period of power-sharing between the Bolshevik Petrograd Soviet and the more liberal provisional government. In October 1917, the Bolsheviks led an armed insurgency of soldiers, sailors, and workers, and seized sole power, thereby establishing Soviet government and, ultimately, the Union of Soviet Socialist Republics (USSR).

intervention into an all-out war against Bolshevik Russia. Nothing came of this, as everyone knows, because his influence was insufficient. Not only Lloyd George but the whole mood of the country was opposed to it. Like the French and Americans, the British had landed a few troops on the Russian coasts in 1918 and lent some rather half-hearted assistance to counter-revolutionary Russian generals. However, their intervention was directed less against the Bolshevik Revolution (although Lenin construed it as such) than against Russia's separate peace with Germany; they wanted somehow to re-establish an eastern front against Germany, but that was all. The end of the war against Germany exhausted their interest in the Russian counter-revolution and, in even greater measure, their appetite for war. Who would voluntarily, for sheer dislike of the Russian Bolsheviks, follow up a long and terrible but ultimately successful war against Germany by making war on Russia? For heaven's sake! Such an idea could only occur to a person who wanted war for war's sake, an insatiable warrior, a lover of bloodshed. All Churchill achieved by waging his intervention campaign was to earn himself that reputation once and for all.

Not entirely without justification, for he really was a man of war. His fellow countrymen quite correctly sensed this, and had already done so, with mixed emotions, in the years before and after 1914. What motivated him in this case, however, was not only his innate delight in war and the art of war, but something elemental: genuine fear and genuine hatred, a feeling that he and his entire world were in unfathomable, terrible, deadly danger. The anti-Bolshevik complex that had taken possession of him in 1918 retained its hold for decades to come.

Bolshevism was far worse than German militarism, he declared in April 1919, and the atrocities committed by Lenin and Trotsky were incomparably more frightful than all the things for which the Kaiser bore responsibility (this at a time when the British public was still in favour of hanging the German emperor). *Bolsheviks, Churchill told Lloyd George, are the enemies of the human race and must be put down at any cost.*

Vladimir Ilyich Ulyanov 'Lenin' (1870–1924), a law graduate from St Petersburg University, became leader of the 'Bolshevik' faction of the Russian Social Democratic Labour Party in 1903. Advocating the creation of a small, disciplined party dedicated to fostering revolution, he spent much of his life imprisoned or in exile. He returned to Russia in the spring of 1917 and took power in the Soviet government that October. He died following a stroke in 1924.

Twenty years later Churchill became renowned for his outrageous command of abusive language. The terrible, cutting, castigating words with which he slapped Hitler and Mussolini across the face reverberated around the world. But they were not the first eruption of such volcanic eloquence; what he found to say of the Bolsheviks in the 1920s had just the same ring. In May 1920 he told the House of Commons *Bolshevism is not a policy; it is a disease. It is not a creed; it is a pestilence.* Bolsheviks were *swarms of typhus-bearing vermin* or *troops of ferocious baboons amid the ruins of cities and the corpses of their victims.* Lenin himself was a *plague bacillus* who wanted to destroy the world.

My view has been that all the harm and misery in Russia have arisen out of the wickedness and folly of the Bolshevists, and that there will be no recovery of any kind in Russia or in Eastern Europe while these wicked men, this vile group of cosmopolitan fanatics, hold the Russian nation by the hair of its head and tyrannize over the great population. The policy I will always

Lev Davidovich Bronstein 'Trotsky' (1879–1940) was a revolutionary, a journalist, and a close companion of Lenin. He returned to Russia in 1917 and played a major role in the Revolution of October 1917. He was then appointed Commissar for War and created the Red Army. Following Lenin's death he was sidelined by Stalin. He was exiled in 1929 and sentenced to death in absentia in 1937. He was murdered in Mexico by Stalin's agents in 1940.

advocate is the overthrow and destruction of that criminal regime.

This was elemental hatred cast in an artistic mould. If words could kill, these would have been lethal, but they fell on deaf ears – indeed, they rebounded on the speaker. To British ears, even British Conservative ears, they sounded unwholesome and overwrought, febrile and rather hysterical.

This impression was all the stronger because Churchill had a manifest tendency to extend his hatred of Bolshevism from foreign to domestic politics, in part to the new and hugely aspiring Labour Party. Socialists and Communists, Communists and Bolsheviks – he deliberately blurred the differences between them; they were all one, all part of the same fatal disease: *Behind Socialism stands Communism, behind Communism stands Moscow, that dark, sinister, evil power.* One begins to understand why Churchill was irresistibly drawn back into the Conservative fold. Early in 1924 the Labour Party had for the first time emerged from an election as the strongest single party, and the Liberals, who held the balance of power, let Labour form the Government for a while – according to Churchill the sort of national disaster to which large countries generally succumb only after losing a war. That, at least, was something the Conservatives would never have done!

One cannot fail to discern that Churchill's reaction to the victory of the Bolshevik Revolution in Russia and the rise of social democratic labour parties in Western Europe – two developments that shaped the post-war world – largely resembled that of the bourgeoisie of Continental Europe, which was then spawning fascism and fascist counter-revolution in one country after another.

Twenty years later it became Churchill's destiny and his historic role to annihilate European fascism in a life-or-death struggle. But anyone who had predicted this in the 1920s would have been rightly laughed to scorn. It seemed much more likely that the Churchill of those years would become European fascism's international figurehead and lead it to sanguinary victory. He was far better suited to the role than Mussolini the socialist renegade or Hitler the plebeian snob. It is no exaggeration or unjust imputation to say that the Churchill of the 1920s was really a fascist; only his nationality precluded him from becoming one in name as well.

Churchill expected the Conservatives to conduct a victorious class struggle and halt the Labour Party's menacing rise as effectively as Italy's Fascists had neutralized the social democrats, albeit by employing the civilized methods of British parliamentary politics. But his party had something else in mind: conciliation, accommodation, pacification. Their response to the social upheavals of wartime and the post-war period differed diametrically from that of the Continental bourgeoisie: it was one of reflection rather than shock. They were determined to play fair with the new political forces and in that way bring them to heel. The Conservatives became appeasers, not fascists – initially in domestic politics.

They outflanked Churchill in a way he found sinister and impalpable, continually shirking the fight he sought. Their objective – never openly proclaimed, but subtly and steadfastly pursued – was not to destroy the new Labour Party, but to adapt and adjust it to the British system: to assimilate, conciliate, and compromise with it until, in the end, the old two-party system would be simply re-established with Labour taking the Liberals' former place. We now know that this objective was triumphantly attained – whether or not to Britain's best advantage is another matter. Perhaps the British still labour under the fact that they were cheated out of a necessary revolution. But that was not, of course, Churchill's objection to Conservative policy.

Churchill, who regarded socialists as unassimilable and civil war as practically inevitable, remained an isolated and unsuccessful figure, and ended by looking rather foolish. It cannot be said that he understood the reasons for his defeat or learned any lessons from them. He became steadily more embittered and entrenched in his views, and by 1930 he had fallen out with the Conservatives once more.

Churchill never understood and was constantly outmanoeuvred by Stanley Baldwin, who was a new species of Conservative leader: not an aristocrat, but the son of a middle-class, provincial manufacturer who knew his workers by name and made a habit of chatting with them in dialect. Baldwin believed in peace between the classes, not class struggle. To him, English workers were not dangerous revolutionaries; they were the Toms, Dicks, and Harrys with whom his father used to joke over a pint of beer. He was an ultra-English, seemingly inarticulate pipe-smoker who combined gentleness and sagacity with quiet cunning. The first thing he did with Churchill after reluctantly taking him back into the Conservative Party was to make him Chancellor of the Exchequer. This hugely prestigious office of state, second only to that of Prime Minister, was also the one Lord Randolph Churchill had held during his brief heyday. Churchill could not possibly decline it. At the same time, it was the government post to which he was least suited. He was completely ignorant of economics and finance –

Stanley Baldwin (1867–1947) served three times as Conservative Prime Minister, 1923–4, 1924–9 and 1935–7. Dominating the Conservative Party for more than a decade, he succeeded in healing the divisions of previous years. He was credited with taking the country back on to the gold standard, defeating the General Strike, and skilfully handling the abdication crisis. After retiring in 1937, he attracted criticism for his support of appeasement, and for his orthodox economic policies.

STANLEY BALDWIN

everyone knew that, himself included – so he would be in the hands of his civil servants. He was flattered, honoured, overwhelmed – and checkmated, just as Baldwin intended.

Churchill remained Conservative Chancellor for five years, from 1924 to 1929, his longest ever tenure of one ministry. Even his glory days at the Admiralty had lasted only three and a half years. His time as Chancellor was not a glorious one, however. He pined for action because his department failed to interest him. Leaving his civil servants to get on with the job, he indulged in his old vice: meddling in the departments of his ministerial colleagues. He was also more of a writer than a minister during this period. *The World Crisis* (1923–9), a five-volume work begun while he was politically on the shelf, was completed during this time. Churchill's egocentric account of the First World War, and possibly his most enthralling work, it was an incredibly audacious but completely successful amalgam of autobiography and history, personal apologia and strategic criticism. The aged former Prime Minister Arthur Balfour called it 'an autobiography disguised as an history of the Universe', but not even he could resist Churchill's spell.

Two important events occurred during Churchill's Chancellorship, both causally related in a way that was obscure at the time: Britain's return to the gold standard and, a year later, the General Strike of May 1926. The return to the gold standard was, in effect, a revaluation of the pound, and its disastrous repercussions on Britain's export industry occasioned the wage cuts and mass unemployment that led to the General Strike. Churchill's department was directly responsible for this revaluation, and the great John Maynard Keynes, then still a young academic outsider and almost alone in finding fault with it, referred to 'the economic consequences of Mr Churchill'. That was unfair, however. The return to the gold standard had been a cabinet decision. Every minister, civil servant, and expert (Keynes apart) was in favour of it, any

THE CHANCELLOR

One of the most influential economists of the twentieth century, John Maynard Keynes (1883–1946) revolutionized economic approaches to handling recession. His radical proposals for dealing with mass unemployment by State intervention and deficit financing enjoyed considerable vogue during and after the Second World War. He was also a critic of the punitive peace imposed on Germany after the First World War.

Conservative Chancellor would have put it into effect, and Churchill, who did not understand it, simply happened to be the Chancellor of the day. It was not his own idea and caused him no special heart-searching.

Not so the General Strike which ensued a year later: for a few days, it seemed to him to herald the great, final battle with the socialist dragon, and all his warrior's instincts were aroused. Baldwin managed to divert and defuse them, however. He entrusted Churchill with the publication of a makeshift government newspaper – all other newspapers had been shut down by the strike – and thus kept him fully occupied. Meanwhile, Baldwin cautiously negotiated with the strikers and settled the dispute within ten days. He later said,

The General Strike, the Brigade of Guards leaving Victoria Park, East London

with a smirk, that this method of neutralizing Winston had been the shrewdest expedient he had ever devised. Churchill's *British Gazette* was a journalistic and organizational achievement of the first order – produced by an amateur staff, it boosted its circulation from zero to two million copies in ten days. At the same time, it was a savagely abusive and provocative

A nine-day stoppage called by the Trades Union Congress (TUC) in May 1926 in support of the miners, the General Strike initially enjoyed almost universal support among the proletariat. However, following a robust response from the Government, which declared the strike unconstitutional and mobilized middle-class volunteers to maintain skeleton services, the TUC abandoned the strike without securing any worthwhile concessions.

rag that gravely damaged Churchill's personal reputation, not only with British workers but also with the moderate and peace-loving middle classes – from Baldwin's point of view, a not unwelcome development.

'Give him enough rope and he'll hang himself.' This was Baldwin's secret formula. He did not fight his opponents; he threw them a rope and watched with quiet compassion while they hanged themselves. He ruined Churchill politically, not by shutting him out, but by giving him a senior though inappropriate government post (and, incidentally, treating him with exquisite courtesy and friendliness). He did the same with the Labour Party and scored his greatest triumph in 1931, when he and its leaders formed a grand coalition. He also did the same with Gandhi's India, which was then clamouring for independence. He contradicted no one and refused nothing, displayed an understanding and accommodating attitude, negotiated, granted a few concessions and promised more, soothed, pacified, disarmed, and – without their really noticing it – transformed rebels into junior partners. He employed these tactics a third time against Hitler's Germany, but they failed, and Churchill proved right in the end.

For Churchill, himself a largely unwitting victim of this policy, was permanently at odds with it. 'Appeasement', whoever its target, was not in his nature. It disgusted him – his whole temperament rebelled against it. He increasingly compromised his position by forever grumbling at Baldwin's masterstroke, internal pacification achieved by the taming of the British Labour Movement – something from which Churchill himself was to profit in a dramatic way. He was outraged that the Viceroy should have received Gandhi, *a seditious Middle Temple lawyer, now posing as a fakir of a type well known in the East, striding half-naked up the steps of the Viceregal palace, while he is still organising and conducting a campaign of civil disobedience.*

Mohandas Karamchand 'Mahatma' Gandhi (1869–1948) was the spiritual father of Indian independence. Educated in London, he returned to India in 1914 where he became leader of the Indian National Congress Party and advocated a policy of peaceful non-cooperation and civil disobedience. After numerous periods of imprisonment, he finally negotiated India's independence in 1947. He was assassinated by a Hindu fanatic the following year.

Early in 1930 Churchill resigned from the Conservative shadow cabinet because of its flexible approach to India (the Conservatives were spending a brief interlude in opposition, with Ramsay MacDonald leading a second Labour government), and for years he delivered caustic speeches condemning their policy of limp acquiescence, self-abasement, and surrender. As time went by this made him a laughing stock. At the age of 55 Churchill was regarded by his fellow countrymen, the Conservatives among them, as a romantic reactionary out of touch with the modern world. They pitied him. So much talent, so much energy – all squandered and come to nothing. He was still an object of interest, still fascinating in his own way, but obviously of no further use. When the Conservatives re-entered government in 1931, they did not offer Churchill a ministerial post, though he remained a Conservative MP. Let him deliver speeches and write books – that was the general view. As a politician to be taken seriously, he was finished.

One against All · 1929–1939

Inactivity was Winston Churchill's personal hell. Even as a minister he had never, or almost never, been completely fulfilled by his work and his responsibilities. He was always a little restless, dissatisfied and indisciplined, always inclined to overflow his banks, meddle in everything, and usurp the authority of others.

For all that, a minister's existence had been just bearable. Being completely marginalized and excluded, compelled to look on while unable to intervene, was unendurable. He had already sampled this intolerable state of affairs more than once in his life: for a dire twelve months from mid-1916 to mid-1917, and for two depressing years from autumn 1922 to autumn 1924. He now had to dwell in this wilderness, this Churchillian hell, for almost a decade: from 1930 to 1939, or from his fifty-fifth to his sixty-fifth year – quite an unexceptional age at which to die.

On the face of it, his life during those ten years was thoroughly agreeable, in fact most people would have thought it enviable. He lived at Chartwell, the rural property in Kent he had acquired with the proceeds of *The World Crisis*. He was always tinkering with the house and garden, sometimes with his own hands, and learnt bricklaying. With an old felt hat on his head, he erected several walls and outbuildings in the sweat of his brow, brick by brick, and insisted on joining the appropriate trade union – a step which its members regarded as something of a bad joke. He planted trees, dug ornamental ponds, fed goldfish, bred exotic varieties of butterflies, travelled, painted. His children, a son and three daughters, were growing up at this period, and he found time to be an interested, warm-hearted and conscientious if rather overbearing father. He once remarked to his son Randolph that they had spoken together more during the school holidays than his father had spoken with him in his entire lifetime. He had many visitors, talked politics until the small hours with friends and strangers, held forth more often than he listened, sometimes drank more than was good for him, and smoked innumerable outsize Havana cigars.

Churchill at work on his *History of the English Speaking Peoples* at Chartwell in 1939

Although out of office, he was far from idle. He pursued a very productive and successful career as a journalist and author. He became what would now be called a columnist, writing a weekly series of articles on international politics. Published in Britain and in many other English-speaking countries, these earned him big fees, and rightly so. What Churchill supplied was first-rate, well-informed, well thought-out journalism, trenchantly expressed, brilliantly formulated, and thoroughly outspoken. But journalism, although his principal source of income, was only a sideline; most of his time was spent on large-scale literary projects. He devoted six years to a four-volume biography of his ancestor, the Duke of Marlborough, which developed into a colossal portrait of the High Baroque period. Old-fashioned in its scope and superabundance, and second only to *The World Crisis* as a crowning literary achievement, this work possesses a visual quality, an ability to conjure up and resurrect, that invites comparison with Thomas Mann's *Joseph* tetralogy, which originated at around the same time. When Churchill had finished *Marlborough, His Life and Times* (1933–8), he set to work on another four-volume work, his *History of the English-Speaking Peoples*. For all its glowing colours and entertainment value, this more clearly reveals his limitations as a historian.

Any other man would have found these activities more than enough in the way of work, play, and *raison d'être*. In Churchill's case they failed even to be an anaesthetic. Yet throughout this period – one could easily forget this salient point – he remained a thoroughly active politician, albeit a shelved and unsuccessful one. He was a hard-working MP throughout these ten years: he delivered many speeches, some of his greatest among them; he sat on various committees; he attached great importance to maintaining contacts inside the Foreign Office and the defence ministries, both sources of inside information; he interpellated and conspired – but all to no measurable effect and without any perceptible success. He had become a hopeless outsider, a lone opponent written off by public opinion and at odds with all three parties, a great man of yesteryear whom one listened to politely and tolerantly, even with a touch of aesthetic admiration, but ignored when it came to the business in hand.

Whatever Churchill did, world history – and British politics – proceeded as if he had never existed. Nothing he said or wrote made the slightest difference, and it is hard to say which plunged him into deeper despair: the course taken by world history – and British politics – which in his view was leading to disaster and disgrace, or his total inability to do anything to change its direction.

To see disaster looming was bad enough; to have to stand idly by, unable to avert it, was probably the worst thing of all. But enforced inactivity might have been worse still without a clear perception of the disasters to come, which revealed at least a secret spark of hope that others would some day be compelled to see how right he was, and that he would be needed once more.

In fact, unbeknown to himself and everyone else, Churchill's ten years in the wilderness enabled him to accumulate the political capital which in 1940 rendered him temporarily all-powerful, unassailable and invulnerable in his capacity as Britain's wartime premier. It was not his youthful brilliance, which was largely forgotten by 1940, nor his role in the First World War, which was still controversial, nor his political activities in the first postwar decade, which even his few friends and admirers found rather embarrassing, but solely the steadfast discernment and fortitude of the lone, admonitory voice crying in the wilderness that suddenly invested him, in 1940, with the reputation of the one man who had been right all along and might still bring national deliverance.

The Churchill of the early 1930s was far from being an antifascist, rather the opposite. Nor, although many people in Germany still think of him as such, was he ever anti-German. He did not love Germany as he loved France and America, but he respected her – even admired her, in a way – and was thoroughly in favour, after both world wars, of welcoming her into the Western bloc as a partner and ally. He did not at first have anything much against Hitler, although he strongly disapproved of his anti-Semitism. It was only as time went by that Churchill developed a genuine distaste for the sinister dictator's cruelty and his peculiar mannerisms, but there was still no question of this in the early 1930s. Indeed, Churchill sometimes expressed the hope that, if Britain ever lost a major war in the same way as Germany had lost the Great War,

Born in Upper Austria, Adolf Hitler (1889–1945) rose from provincial obscurity to become German dictator. After service in the First World War, he joined the nascent National Socialist German Workers' Party (NSDAP) in Munich in 1919. As one of a number of 'new' political parties in post-war Germany, the NSDAP was in essence a populist, nationalist party with a strongly anti-Semitic and anti-Communist character. In 1923, Hitler led the party in an abortive putsch, for which he was imprisoned. After refounding the party in 1925, he won a series of election victories in 1930 and 1932, culminating in his appointment as Chancellor in 1933. Thereafter, he rapidly established a dictatorship and one-party State. He led Germany into the Second World War in 1939 and committed suicide when Berlin fell to the Soviet army in 1945.

a Hitler would arise there too, and in 1932 he would have been quite prepared to meet Hitler socially while visiting Munich on the track of Marlborough's march to the Danube.

No, there were at first quite different reasons, far from dishonourable but far more worldly and politically tactical, for the fact that Churchill became the great advocate of British rearmament from 1932 onwards – increasingly so in 1934, 1935, and 1936 – and that he necessarily, in the same context, became the great Cassandra where German rearmament was concerned. Strictly speaking, he slid into his hostility to Nazism, as it were, only because he was temperamentally opposed to a policy of appeasement, and because the Nazis – after the Labour Party and the Indians – had

ADOLF HITLER

Adolf Hitler

now become the object of that policy on Britain's part. It is also possible that his brief personal contact with the Nazi movement in Munich in 1932 had awakened and alarmed him at some deeper level; being himself a warrior by blood and instinct, he probably recognized a warlike atmosphere – scented it, so to speak – when he encountered one. What was more immediately important, however, was that he badly needed a cause and a topic that could reconcile him with the Conservative Party and offer him the prospect of a return to power and ministerial office. The rearmament question promised to be just that.

Most Conservatives were not instinctive disarmers, pacifism or the League of Nations ideology being more characteristic of the Left. At heart, the vast majority of Conservatives had always favoured reliance on a policy of strength, so a robust appeal to that sentiment could be expected to fall on fertile soil. In fact, Churchill briefly regained a little influence in 1934 and 1935 by making such an appeal. In the spring of 1936 – Hitler had already introduced universal conscription and occupied the Rhineland – the Conservative government decided to adopt a

Established at the Treaty of Versailles (1919), the League of Nations was foreseen as an organization to preserve peace by the prevention or consensual settlement of international disputes. Although it succeeded in settling a number of minor disputes, it was increasingly ineffective in the late 1930s, especially when faced with the concerted aggression of Japan, Italy, and Nazi Germany. Its functions were transferred to the United Nations in 1946.

cautious rearmament policy and created a ministerial post responsible for defence co-ordination. Churchill seemed the ideal, almost inescapable choice, but Baldwin passed him over. He had no wish to overdo rearmament, nor, probably, to have a troublemaker in the Cabinet.

This hit Churchill hard. It was doubtless only then that he suspected, or realized, that he had burnt his boats with the Conservatives – that there was no way back, and that they simply didn't want him any more.

The same year, 1936, brought another terrible confirmation of this suspicion (or realization): an extremely embarrassing incident that revealed in a flash how completely his ties with the world of contemporary British politics had been severed. He underwent an experience to which no one else had been subjected in living memory: he was booed and shouted down in Parliament.

It happened in connection with Edward VIII's abdication, which Churchill was trying to prevent or at least postpone – a remarkable and not uncharacteristic episode. Everyone knows the celebrated story of Edward VIII's passionate affair with the twice divorced, still married American, and remembers the cruel ultimatum that Baldwin presented to the young King in the late autumn of 1936: either give up the only woman he had ever been able to love, or renounce the throne.

Edward VIII (1894–1972) was King of the United Kingdom from January to December 1936. His desire to marry the American divorcée Wallis Simpson precipitated the abdication crisis and caused him to relinquish the crown in favour of his brother, George VI. Edward was temporarily Governor of Bermuda, but lived most of his life in exile in France.

We are, of course, entitled to our own opinion of the old-fashioned, somewhat hypocritical puritanism of the contemporary British establishment. But if we take it as given and concede that the Britain of 1936 could never have accepted as queen a multiple divorcée whose liaison with the

THE ABDICATION CRISIS

The Duke and Duchess of Windsor

King had started while she was still married to another man, we must also concede that Baldwin's enforcement of a quick decision was the only possible course of action. What could Churchill have hoped to achieve by advocating leniency and postponement on the grounds that it would be at least six months before the then Mrs Simpson's decree nisi became absolute? What would have changed in those six months? The moral perceptions of the British ruling class? Churchill himself could not have believed that. The King's feelings? That might have been possible had this been the passing fancy of an exuberantly sensual man. But Churchill knew full well that something quite different was involved, something deeper and more delicate, something in the nature of deliverance, and that the King would never give up a woman who had miraculously granted him access to the opposite sex. So what was to be gained by postponing the issue? Only embarrassment, only prolonged mental torment, only months of intolerable public prying into the most intimate areas of the King's private life; only, last but not least, the undermining and imperilling of the monarchy itself. There is no doubt that Baldwin was right and Churchill wrong.

No doubt, either, that Baldwin's approach was as cold and heartless as Churchill's was warm-hearted, magnanimous, and chivalrous. Churchill always took a generous attitude in matters of the heart, and besides, he cherished a kind of feudal loyalty to his youthful, harassed sovereign. But that was just what the British public refused to accept. Knowing Churchill as they thought they did, they took him for a man of demonic, unscrupulous ambition who now, in despair at being shut out, balked at absolutely nothing. They also saw him as hopelessly obsolete, an old-fashioned warrior who was capable, if given his head, of rekindling not only a world war but even an English civil war. King versus Parliament with Churchill at the head of a 'king's party' – such were the memories and fears to which people seriously yielded when he made his lone intervention in the abdication crisis. That was why they briefly abandoned their parliamentary dignity and shouted him down. This may have been the moment at which it first became patently obvious, not only to Churchill but to those around him, what an utter foreign body he had become in the Britain of 1936.

Such was the state of affairs, and such the extent to which relations between Churchill and the British political establishment had deteriorated, when in 1937, despite his incessant, despairing protests and ominous predictions, the Government initiated a policy of public rapprochement towards Germany – a policy designed to bring peace but destined to lead to war.

The Government changed its leader in May 1937. Having domi-nated politics for 15 years with lordly self-assurance, Baldwin went into voluntary, dignified retirement, a much respected and eulo-gized figure. His replacement by Neville Chamberlain betokened no change of policy but a complete change of style. Baldwin had

Neville Chamberlain (1869–1940) was Conservative Prime Minister from 1937 to 1940. Representing constituencies in his native Birmingham from 1918, he held a number of posts, including Minister of Health (1924–9) and Chancellor of the Exchequer (1931–37), before succeeding Baldwin as Prime Minister. Largely outmanoeuvred by Hitler in foreign affairs, Chamberlain reluctantly led the country into war in 1939, but a motion of no confidence after the disastrous Norwegian campaign the following year ended his career.

been a soft, corpulent, bulky man; Chamberlain was lean, almost gaunt, and his fine-boned frame combined hardness with delicacy. The two men's political style precisely matched their physical appearance. Both were peacemakers, and both cherished a profound belief that careful doses of flexibility can be an irresistible political weapon more cogent and disarming than obdurate resistance. Baldwin preferred to leave matters vague and indeterminate for as long as possible, however, whereas Chamberlain was, in his own way, a man of action given to tidying things and setting them in order. Meticulous and consistently calculating, he laid his plans in advance and was firmly resolved to act too soon rather than too late.

Baldwin had tended to avoid a head-on confrontation with Hitler; Chamberlain sought one almost immediately. As early as autumn 1937 he sent Lord Halifax – later his Foreign Secretary and the man who had pacified Gandhi as Viceroy of India – to Germany to obtain a clear picture of Hitler's aims. He was secretly determined, even at that stage and however much it hurt the many people affected, to grant Hitler every possible concession. Far from

Edward Wood (1881–1959), 6th Earl of Halifax, was a Conservative politician and diplomat. He served as Viceroy of India (1926–31) and later as Foreign Secretary (1938–40), when he became a staunch supporter of Chamberlain's policy of appeasement. Though considered as a candidate to succeed Chamberlain, he backed Churchill's accession and subsequently served as ambassador to the United States.

being soft, his peace policy was as bone hard as the man himself.

Was it fundamentally mistaken from the first? Churchill spent three years utterly condemning Chamberlain's policy, which he regarded as disgraceful, ruinous folly and weakness. Was he entirely right and Chamberlain wrong? That has been the general view among post-war historians. But during those three years – 1937, 1938, and 1939 – public opinion, at least in Britain, was firmly convinced of the opposite. In the interests of historical justice, the reasons for this are still worth examining.

First, Chamberlain had a far better appreciation of Britain's economic and financial circumstances than Churchill, who always brushed this aspect of things aside in a rather cavalier manner. A long-serving and, unlike Churchill, extremely proficient and successful Chancellor of the Exchequer, Chamberlain knew that Britain had exhausted her reserves in the Great War, and that a second such war, even if she emerged victorious, would spell disaster for her economy and finances, and thus for her now precarious status as a world power – an assessment that proved to be correct. Churchill refused to see that large-scale rearmament was really beyond Britain's means. Even allowing for its awful unpredictability, another world war was something to be avoided at almost any price if Britain did not want to bankrupt herself.

And was it really unavoidable? Germany's resurrection as a great military power could no longer be prevented; by 1937 it was an accomplished fact. But did this new Germany absolutely have to be an enemy of Britain? What did Hitler really want? Colonies, too, of course – an awkward and embarrassing matter – but his principal objectives were quite different: Austria, the Sudetenland, Danzig, the Polish Corridor, Upper Silesia. Taken together, these would naturally entail German domination of the whole of Central and Eastern Europe. Chamberlain realized this as clearly as Churchill, but was it really such an unacceptable threat as Churchill took for granted? If Britain assisted Germany in her endeavours and voluntarily helped her to acquire all she wanted, wouldn't that establish peace between Britain and Germany at least for a while, possibly for quite a long while, possibly 'in our time'? And wouldn't it satiate Germany herself, rendering her sluggish, lazy, and peaceable?

The Union of Soviet Socialist Republics (USSR) was a federation of 15 republics established in 1923 following the Bolshevik Revolution. A dictatorship of the Communist Party, it enjoyed rapid industrial growth but laboured under a repressive regime, especially under Stalin. Victorious in the Second World War, it expanded its political influence into Central and Eastern Europe to create the Soviet Bloc. In the subsequent Cold War, it scored some successes, but ultimately failed to keep pace with the democratic West, especially the United States. The USSR was formally dissolved in 1991.

And even if it did not, with whom would her still unassuaged expansionism bring her into conflict – always assuming that it really was still unassuaged? With Britain? With the French and the Dutch, whom Britain could certainly never abandon? No, obviously with Russia – with the Bolshevik Russia against which Churchill himself had wanted to reinforce Germany less than 20 years ago! Chamberlain was unwilling even to do that. For all his deep-seated mistrust of Moscow, he was no anti-Communist crusader like Churchill. But if a large-scale clash eventually occurred between Germany and Russia, quite of its own accord and without his assistance, would that be so very intolerable from Britain's point of view? What if she looked on in the role of referee, quietly rearming and husbanding her strength, and finally preserved the loser in a Russo-German war from destruction? Mightn't that be a most advantageous position?

Lastly, with whom did Churchill propose to build up his intimidatory coalition, and, if intimidation failed, his war coalition against Hitler's Germany? America was disarmed and isolationist. France, bled white by the Great War, was even more nervously intent on peace and security than Britain. Russia? Stalin's crisis-torn Russia, which was currently preoccupied with exterminating her entire general staff? In default of all these, a ragbag of small,

Iosif Vissarionovich Dzhugashvili 'Stalin' (1879–1953) was born in Georgia the son of a cobbler. Involved in the revolutionary underground from an early age, he played an active role in the Bolshevik Revolution and was a member of the first 'Politburo'. After Lenin's death he gradually asserted control to become dictator of the USSR. After an uneasy alliance with Nazi Germany in 1939, he became an ally of the United States and Britain when attacked by Hitler in 1941. He oversaw the expansion of Soviet power into Central and Eastern Europe in the aftermath of the Second World War and, with that, the early stages of the Cold War.

WAR AGAINST GERMANY

weak, threatened, frightened European countries? A ludicrous idea – not even Churchill could seriously entertain it! Unpredictable as ever, he chose this moment to discover the League of Nations and collective security, thereby gaining a few surprised and reluctant sympathizers on the Left. Chamberlain could only shrug his shoulders in annoyance at this.

Retracing these lines of thought, we can understand why Churchill's warnings, which now read so prophetically, went completely unheeded, whereas Chamberlain briefly won greater renown as a realistic and ruthless peacemaker than any British statesman for centuries. We cannot help wondering where Churchill found the immense store of self-belief that enabled him to endure the total isolation, indeed, ostracism, to which he was subjected year after year. He had now truly become, in the world of British politics, what he had once been in the equally inescapable toils of the British educational system half a century before: utterly out of place, utterly alone, fighting a losing battle, friendless, secretly disconsolate, an impotent rebel repeatedly beaten but repeatedly raising his voice in protest. The relatively hopeful political tactics with which he had conducted his rearmament campaign a few years earlier were a thing of the past. He now knew that every dire prediction he uttered only made him less acceptable. It must have been an eerie, nerve-racking realization that his only mainstay and only hope lay in the certainty of disaster. That certainty he did possess, however. And, as everyone knows, it was well founded.

What was it that made him right? What did Churchill see clearly that Chamberlain, who was so much shrewder and more calculating, misinterpreted or failed to see at all? The answer consists of a single word, a single name: Hitler.

Hitler did not enter into Chamberlain's calculations, so to speak. His place in them was occupied by an abstraction: a German statesman who assessed his country's prospects and interests as soberly and rationally as Chamberlain assessed those of Britain. With such a partner, Chamberlain's policy could not have failed; with a partner like Hitler, it did not stand a chance.

Hitler not only took it for granted that concessions were a sign of weakness and cowardice and an invitation to kick those who granted them; he was a man who craved war for war's sake – or, rather, for the sake of his real aim, the biological revolution which war alone could bring about. He was not a statesman, either; he thought in terms of races, not states. The German interests Chamberlain so carefully built into his calculations were fundamentally immaterial to Hitler, who openly said as much in 1945, just before the end. For him, Germany was the tool with which he sought to carry out his very own brand of world revolution: the extermination of the Jews, the enslavement of the Slavs, and the breeding of a new Germanic master race.

All this completely surpassed Chamberlain's powers of comprehension. To him, a phenomenon like Hitler was wholly unfathomable – unthinkable, in fact. There is no doubt that Churchill's understanding of Hitler was also incomplete, but it sufficed for practical purposes. He grasped that Hitler wanted war, and that concessions merely encouraged him to lash out. Churchill understood, if only by degrees, that Hitler was not a normal statesman but an extremely sinister species of revolutionary – in Churchill's eyes, no less sinister than the Bolsheviks of 1918, so it was easy for him to transfer his elemental hatred of Lenin and Trotsky to the German dictator.

As we all know, people cannot understand a thing unless they have a little of it within themselves. Churchill was an infinitely finer, nobler, and more humane figure than Hitler – morally and aesthetically as far removed from him as Blenheim Palace was from the men's hostel in Vienna's Meldemannstrasse. Yet it was no mere accident that transformed those two men, the superior and

The end of the wilderness years. Churchill returns to Parliament, 1939

the inferior, into each other's destiny. For that was what they became. But for Churchill, Hitler would have triumphed, and but for Hitler, Churchill would have died a brilliant, anachronistic failure. Unbeknown to either of them and without their ever meeting in the flesh, the two men had for years been on a collision course that ended in their duel to the death. They belonged together, in a certain sense, just as they will always belong together in history.

Although utterly dissimilar, they did have three qualities in common: the warlike – both were born for war and revelled in it; the anachronistic – neither really belonged in the twentieth century, but in earlier, more violent times; and the extreme – both of them, each in his very different way, went to the very limit in certain directions, withered away in temperate zones where others thrived, and sprang to life only when others flagged.

These considerations must take the place of an account of Chamberlain's appeasement policy and its failure, for which there is no room here. Suffice it to say that it failed – increasingly so as the initiative passed from Chamberlain to Hitler. This process began in September 1938. It continued, haltingly at first, then gathered speed at an ultimately breathtaking rate until, twelve months later, Chamberlain abruptly and almost incomprehensibly found himself embroiled in a war with Hitler – the war it had been the whole aim of his policy to avert.

With just the same rapidity – almost imperceptibly at first, then ever faster – Churchill's star resumed its ascent as 1939 progressed. It was Hitler who enabled it to rise. As Chamberlain noted in the summer of 1939, Churchill's chances improved as war became more of a possibility.

Britain declared war on Germany on 3 September. The same day, Chamberlain recalled Churchill to government. He was given his old post, the one in which he had entered the First World War a quarter of a century earlier: First Lord of the Admiralty. The Board of the Admiralty made the following radio signal to all Royal Navy warships: 'Winston is back.'

Déjà vu · 1939–1940

One of Churchill's first official acts – the war less than two weeks old – was to visit the Home Fleet at Scapa Flow.

Compared to the fleet at his disposal 25 years earlier, it had shrunk after two decades of naval disarmament. When the admiral in command took him on board his flagship, it struck Churchill that the huge vessel was sailing naked, so to speak, without any escorting destroyers. It was customary to have at least two, even for a single battleship. Of course, the admiral replied, that was what he would have liked, but he simply didn't have enough destroyers.

Churchill's thoughts went back a quarter of a century to that other September when he had last visited Sir John Jellicoe and his captains in that same bay, and had found them with their long lines of battleships and cruisers drawn up at anchor. Much had changed. Most of the captains and admirals he had met then were now dead or retired, and Churchill was surrounded by new faces. *The perfect discipline, style and bearing, the ceremonial routine – all were unchanged. But an entirely different generation filled the uniforms and the posts.* Only the ships were the same. *It was a strange experience, like suddenly resuming a previous incarnation . . . If we were in fact going over the same cycle a second time, should I have once again to endure the pangs of dismissal?*

And what of the battle ahead? *Poland in its agony; France but a pale reflection of her former warlike ardour; the Russian Colossus no longer an ally, not even neutral, possibly to become a foe. Italy no friend. Japan no ally. Would America ever come in again? The British Empire remained intact and gloriously united, but ill-prepared, unready.* She still had command of the sea, but she was woefully outmatched in numbers in the air.

There are two rare but incredibly unsettling phenomena familiar enough to the reader of romantic fiction but hard to cope with by those who come across them in reality: the doppelgänger or double, and *déjà vu* – an encounter with oneself and an equally alarming and unnerving encounter with one's own past. Seldom has fate played a more unfathomably sinister joke on anyone than on the superstitious man that Churchill still secretly was. He found himself transported 25 years back into the past – back into precisely the same old traumatic situation he had never forgotten or come to terms with: the time of his highest hopes and cruellest, most abject downfall. Once again he was the supreme naval authority, and once again war had broken out, but the picture was very much darker, more ominous and critical than it had been then: the fleet far smaller and weaker, the military situation far less promising, he himself far older, and even the Government to which he had suddenly been recalled, from one day to the next, far less homely and familiar. His new colleagues had all until recently been his political enemies. Prime Minister Chamberlain was no paternally ironical patron like Asquith, but a very uncongenial person with whom Churchill had never got on, and by whom he had never been treated with anything save mistrust, dislike, and a kind of quiet contempt (which he reciprocated).

Churchill's weird feeling of *déjà vu* did not subside after his visit to the fleet at Scapa Flow in September 1939. It persisted and renewed itself throughout the nine long and depressing months that elapsed between then and May 1940. In retrospect, he may have seen this as a last, drastic test, a rigorous examination to which destiny – with which he maintained an old, intimate, atavistically religious relationship – had submitted his mental fibre before finally disclosing what it had in mind for him; before finally giving him his head, finally permitting him to show what he was made of and what he could do. While the nightmare of déjà vu persisted, however, no one including Churchill could tell what its sequel would be. Being superstitious, he may have expected it to endure to the bitter end and culminate in a second, terrible, final fall from grace.

One did not, in fact, have to be superstitious to anticipate this. Far more so than a quarter of a century earlier, sober reality suggested that 'great ships would be sunk and things go wrong'; and this time around Churchill knew in advance how First Lords of the Admiralty were treated in such cases. It would have been thoroughly excusable, indeed, almost natural, if his behaviour had resembled that of the burnt child who dreads fire: hesitant, cautious, temporizing, safety-conscious. It did not. His daemon proved stronger than his fear. With the experience of 1914–15 before his eyes and its trauma etched deep into his soul, he behaved exactly as he had then – and everything went just as wrong. The name of his new Dardanelles was Norway.

Strangely enough, however, what had then been his ruin now became his salvation. After the failure of the Dardanelles operation, everyone except Churchill had survived the political settlement of accounts. This time, after the failure of the Norway campaign, he was the only one who survived its political repercussions. Everything collapsed around him; he alone remained unscathed. He was just as guilty and innocent of the débâcle as he had been then. Then he had been sent packing; this time he became Prime Minister.

The Western Front had congealed once more. No Allied offensive would be practicable for a long time to come, and it was hoped that a German offensive had equally little prospect of success. At all events, there was nothing to be done but sit tight and prepare for it as carefully as possible.

But was there really nothing to be done in the meantime? The majority of the War Cabinet inclined to that view. Not so Churchill. It went against the grain with him to declare war and then fail to wage it properly. He instinctively felt, and rightly so, that prolonged inactivity proves wearing, crippling, and lethal. As in 1914, so in 1939, he also possessed strategic imagination – too much of it, perhaps. Where others saw nothing, he discerned openings and possibilities, weak points at which the enemy could be dealt a blow. *We still had command of the sea.* Didn't that still confer mobility, omnipresence, and the ability to launch surprise attacks? Were there no points at which the enemy was vulnerable, places accessible to the long arm of the Royal Navy but not to Germany, the ponderous, land-based power?

As in the First World War, Churchill's searching strategic gaze roamed the outlying seas, islands, and peninsulas of Europe. They, far more than the central land mass, seemed to him to present openings for a specifically British strategy based on sea power.

Twenty-five years earlier his eyes had come to rest on the Dardanelles. This time he thought he detected a strategic opening at the opposite extremity of the map, in the far north of Norway.

The Germans' great weakness, everyone agreed in 1939, was their precarious war economy. They lacked many strategically important raw materials – notably iron ore, for which they were dependent on supplies from the far north of Sweden. In summer these came via the Baltic, which was out of Britain's reach, but autumn had now come and the Baltic would soon be ice-bound. In the winter Swedish iron ore had to be transported via the Lofoten railway to the north Norwegian port of Narvik, and then by ship down Norway's jagged coast to Germany. But facing Norway in Scotland was the British fleet.

What if it launched a surprise attack, mined the skerries, and took Narvik by means of a sudden attack? A questionable act in terms of international law, true, although certain precedents existed from the First World War (they would have to be consulted), but what a brilliant opportunity to paralyse the very source of Germany's steel and arms production!

Churchill broached his idea to the War Cabinet as early as 19 September. Ten days later he followed it up with an exhaustive memorandum. Almost simultaneously, on 3 October, Admiral Erich Raeder submitted to Hitler a preliminary plan for the occupation of bases in Norway, its purpose being to secure supplies of iron ore. Unbeknown to each other, German and British staff officers worked throughout the winter on very similar plans, all of them directed at Norway. The difference was, the Germans worked faster.

What is deducible from this difference in speed is not only the greater extent of British scruples, but simply the advantage a dictator has in wartime over a collective cabinet. It is not unfair to assume that Churchill was aware primarily of the latter handicap. It is clear from his memoirs, written years later, how irked he was by the discussions that dragged on for months until the whole venture had lost its strategic point; by decisions half taken and then revoked, by the toing and froing, the compromises, the compulsion to argue where he would have liked to decide a thing and order it to be done. It was an exact repetition of what had happened when the Dardanelles operation was being mounted in 1915, except that this time co-operation between the navy and the army, which had then been very inadequate, did not work at all.

Norway in 1940 turned out to be an even greater, swifter, and more humiliating defeat than the Dardanelles had been in 1915. It was a setback for which Churchill, if strictly honest, was even less entitled to acquit himself of blame or joint responsibility. The Dardanelles operation had been a good strategic idea ruined in practice. The Norway operation contained an inherent strategic flaw from the outset: it failed to take account of the impotence of

The Norwegian Campaign, British soldiers captive in Trondheim

naval power in the face of superior enemy air power. On 9 April, when it became clear that the Germans had stolen a march on the British in Norway, Churchill was exultant. *We have them where we wanted them,* he declared in Cabinet. He thought the Royal Navy could cut off the German troops that had been transported up the North Sea coast. He failed to see that the Germans had now occupied Norway's airfields, and that a fleet could not operate beneath skies dominated by enemy bombers. (It was not a modern fleet of aircraft carriers, but still largely a fleet of battleships, Churchill's old fleet from the First World War.)

By 2 May 1940 the failure of the Norwegian expedition was past concealing. On 7 and 8 May the House of Commons sat in judgement on it. On 10 May the Germans launched their all-out offensive on the Western Front. That same day, Chamberlain resigned and Churchill became Prime Minister.

97

It was 25 years, almost to the day, since Churchill had entered Asquith's office and sustained the terrible blow of dismissal. This time, what had then blighted his political career brought him supreme power. Boundless and unjust punishment on the first occasion, a boundless (and equally unmerited) reward on the second – for the same thing. The unpredictable, blind, and capricious outcome of political roulette, or the cryptic, unfathomable workings of fate?

One can take a close-up view of the drama of those days in May 1940 and see it as the complex political intrigue it superficially was; it then becomes a tragicomedy in which punishments and rewards were meted out in a highly arbitrary way. Or one can take a long-range view and see it simply but vaguely as a decision made by 'Britain', a popular consensus; then everything becomes meaningful, just, and clear-cut – but also insusceptible of proof.

Briefly summarized, developments on the political stage had taken the following course. Chamberlain in 1940, like Asquith in 1915, headed a one-party government. The Labour and Liberal parties were in opposition, just as the Labour and Conservative parties had been then. Now, as then, there were practical arguments in favour of a grand coalition. In a war that promises to be long and hard-fought and has opened with a series of setbacks, no country can afford party politics in the long run. But Chamberlain, unlike Asquith 25 years earlier, was unacceptable as Prime Minister to the current opposition parties. He had made too many enemies. A grand coalition entailed a new premier.

Who could replace Chamberlain? It could only be a Conservative because the Conservatives still commanded a large parliamentary majority. Chamberlain's own candidate to succeed him was his Foreign Secretary, Lord Halifax, who seemed in many ways a more suitable successor than Churchill. Halifax was a man without enemies, an advocate of compromise and conciliation. Jointly responsible for appeasement, he had distanced himself from it sooner and more skilfully than Chamberlain and was thoroughly representative of the transition from appeasement to military preparedness. To the opposition parties he was in many respects

Churchill with Halifax. The former Foreign Secretary was soon to take up the important post of Ambassador to the United States of America

more acceptable than Churchill, whose reactionary period had not been forgotten.

Being a peer, however, Halifax sat in the House of Lords, and it had for 40 years been an unwritten rule that the Prime Minister had to sit in the House of Commons. Although this problem might have been surmounted in such exceptional times, what counted against him more was the very fact of his being a man of compromise and conciliation, not a man of war. And there was a war on.

This was where superficial, politically tactical considerations gave way to the vague but really decisive ulterior motives that took effect at this time. Not even the politicians who based their tactical calculations on who would serve in a coalition government were deaf to the indefinable but unmistakable whispers of the collective subconscious to which every Briton was exposed during those days and weeks.

Formulated with the benefit of hindsight, these whispers ran roughly as follows: Chamberlain is a man of peace, but he has shot his bolt. He wanted peace, but what came of his efforts was war, and war is not his forte. Although worthy, Lord Halifax is a flexible man, a man given to compromise and accommodation, an equivocal man. Having neatly engineered his own transition from peace to war, he might be capable of retracing his steps with equal grace and dignity. If we lost the war, he might be the right person to obtain a reasonable, tolerable peace settlement. But is that what we want? Is the war already lost? Hell, no! First let's see if it can still be won. What Britain needs for the moment is a fighter.

And there's one to hand: Churchill. Churchill is a fighter who loves war. Not only did he positively enjoy the First World War; he would have liked to wage war against Russia in 1919 and Turkey in 1922, and he would probably, if we'd let him, have launched the present war against Germany back in 1935 or 1936 or 1938. We've never given him the helm precisely because he is a man of war. We now need such a man – he's the right one for the job. Forget the Dardanelles and Norway. He may have made mistakes, but he's a fighter and we're at war. Let him show what he's made of. Perhaps he can pull us through. (If not, there's still time for Halifax.)

'Britain' hadn't wanted the war she firmly believed Churchill had always wanted, but now she had it; ergo, let Churchill wage it. In those days, that was the rudimentary and unspoken but prevailing basic idea that bore Churchill upwards, swamping and overwhelming any more superficial considerations.

In the division on 8 May, more than 30 Conservatives joined the opposition parties in voting against the Government, and more than 60 abstained. Chamberlain promptly and selflessly decided to resign. For two days he continued to fight for Lord Halifax's succession, but the scales were already tipping in Churchill's favour when, on the morning of 10 May, Hitler finally clinched matters by launching his grand offensive in the West – another example of the almost occult way in which the two men's destinies were linked. Hitler had summoned Churchill back on to the political stage in 1939; now, on 10 May 1940, he ordained that Churchill should become Prime Minister. Chamberlain abandoned his resistance to Churchill the same day, and it was he who loyally rallied the still recalcitrant Conservative majority behind him.

Chamberlain's personal tragedy is worth a brief glance. At the beginning of September, when the Cabinet resolved at his suggestion to prepare Britain for a war of at least three years' duration, he rested his head on the table top in front of him. When he looked up again, he was deathly pale. He found the thought of three years of war unbearable, yet it was he who had put the motion. Similarly, it was he who resolved that he should be succeeded by his antipode and antitype, Churchill the warrior, and who became his staunchest supporter.

No one but Chamberlain could have commended Churchill to

the bulk of the Conservatives, with their old, profound, and in many cases inherited mistrust of him, in that terrible summer of 1940. He did so steadfastly and selflessly, without flinching, but it broke him. He relinquished his office to Churchill on 10 May. On 16 June he suddenly collapsed with stomach pains. One month later he was found to have cancer. He remained a minister under Churchill for another three months. By 9 November he was dead.

Churchill played little part in the crisis that made him Prime Minister. He had done his best to defend the Government in the House of Commons on 8 May, when old Lloyd George, intervening in a major debate for the last time, warned Churchill that he 'must not allow himself to be converted into an air-raid shelter to keep the splinters from hitting his colleagues'. When Chamberlain summoned him and Lord Halifax to discuss the succession, Churchill said nothing. He yearned for power with every fibre of his being, of course, but he was superstitious and a burnt child. Churchill had no wish to ruin his chances. He was a fatalist, too, and he may have felt that destiny, which had teased and toyed with but preserved him for so long, was now, at long last, showing what it had preserved him for, and that he need do no more. His hour had come. As he recorded in a celebrated passage in his war memoirs:

I was conscious of a profound sense of relief. At last I had the authority to give directions over the whole scene. I felt as if I were walking with destiny, and that all my past life had been but a preparation for this hour and for this trial. Eleven years in the political wilderness had freed me from ordinary Party antagonisms. My warnings over the last six years had been so numerous, so detailed, and were now so terribly vindicated, that no one could gainsay me. I could not be reproached either for making the war or with want of preparation for it. I thought I knew a good deal about it all, and I was sure I should not fail. Therefore, although impatient for the morning, I slept soundly and had no need for cheering dreams. Facts are better than dreams.

The Man of Destiny · 1940–1942

It would be quite possible to delete the figure of Churchill from the pre-1940 history of the world, and even of Britain, without decisively altering the general picture: a single facet would be missing, nothing more. The same is true after 1942. If Churchill had succumbed to the pneumonia that confined him to bed at Carthage on his return from the Teheran Conference in the winter of 1943–4, it would have made no essential difference. The gigantic nutcracker whose steel jaws crushed Hitler's Germany and occupied Europe in 1945 was already closing, and would have functioned just as efficiently without Churchill as with him.

But in 1940 and 1941 Churchill was the man of destiny. Those were the years when his career melded with the history of the world, and neither can be recounted without the other. Without Churchill, the story of those crucial years would be different. No one can tell how it would have turned out.

Might there, but for Churchill, have been a compromise peace settlement or armistice between Britain and Germany in the autumn of 1940 or the summer of 1941? Although there is no way of proving it, the possibility cannot be discounted. Might Hitler, with his rear secured, have defeated Russia as planned? Maybe, maybe not. Considering the knife-edge situation that prevailed outside Moscow in October 1941, one is inclined to say: Yes, probably. But for Churchill, would America have entered the war against Germany? Or rather, without Churchill's crucial impetus and steadfast assistance, would Roosevelt have committed America against Germany in the way he did? It is doubtful.

Ultimately, of course, it was not Churchill's Britain alone that broke Germany's back and laid Hitler low. She was not strong enough for that; for that she needed an alliance with the two giants, America and Russia. Nonetheless, had it not been for Britain's grim determination while standing alone between June 1940 and June 1941, that highly incongruous alliance might never have come about. Moreover, without Churchill, Britain might not have been so grimly determined.

In short, but for Churchill in 1940 and 1941, it is quite conceivable that Hitler might have won the war and would have founded a Greater Germanic SS state extending from the Atlantic to the Urals or beyond. But for Churchill, too, it is possible that the British Empire would still exist (Hitler was very keen to preserve it), albeit as an uneasy partner of Hitler's Eurasian continental empire, and probably in a very fascistic and barbaric form. The worldwide counter-revolution with which Churchill himself had so often flirted during the 1920s might – without him – have triumphed, at least in the short term. One cannot even exclude the possibility that Hitler's war of retribution and subjugation against America, a war he hoped to lead at the head of the Old World after colonizing Russia, might since have been fought and won by Greater Germany in alliance with the British Empire.

But Churchill existed, so world history took a different course. Thanks to him, Britain threw herself in the path of Hitler's break-through at the crucial moment, when his triumph was almost complete. This was against Britain's own best interests, strictly speaking, since she risked not only her physical existence but the basis of her economic and imperial existence as well. In the event, she successfully preserved her physical existence but lastingly ruined her economy and lost her empire.

Although Churchill did not wish this to happen, he was prepared to accept it if the worst came to the worst. He believed and hoped that he would be able to avert these dangers, strove hard and ingeniously to do so, but failed: that was his tragedy. One thing he did want – at any price, if need be: the total, unconditional defeat of Hitler and Hitler's Germany. That he did achieve, and that was his triumph.

In his very first parliamentary speech as Prime Minister, the famous *I have nothing to offer but blood, toil, tears and sweat* speech of 13 May 1940, Churchill declared that his policy was simply to wage war – war *against a monstrous tyranny never surpassed in the dark, lamentable catalogue of human crime*; and that his sole aim was *victory, victory at all costs, victory in spite of all terror, victory, however long and hard the road may be; for without victory there is no survival.* Many of his

The withdrawal from Dunkirk, British troops on an improvised pier of motor vehicles awaiting evacuation, 1940

audience – level-headed, hard-boiled British MPs who listened to him relatively unmoved and without indulging in any frantic ovations – may have mistaken this for the baroque Churchillian rhetoric to which they were accustomed. Events were to prove him in deadly earnest.

A few weeks later, in June 1940, he made his meaning even

BLOOD, TOIL, TEARS AND SWEAT

plainer. After the retreat from Dunkirk, when everyone was briefly uncertain whether Hitler's next move would be directed at tottering France or largely defenceless Britain, Churchill told Parliament:

Even though large tracts of Europe and many old and famous States have fallen or may fall into the grip of the Gestapo and all the odious apparatus of Nazi rule, we shall not flag or fail.

We shall go on to the end. We shall fight in France, we shall fight on the seas and oceans, we shall fight with growing confidence and growing strength in the air, we shall defend our island, whatever the cost may be.

We shall fight on the beaches, we shall fight on the landing grounds, we shall fight in the fields and in the streets, we shall fight in the hills; we shall never surrender.

And even if, which I do not for a moment believe, this island or a large part of it were subjugated and starving, then our Empire beyond the seas, armed and guarded by the British Fleet, would carry on the struggle, until, in God's good time, the New World, with all its power and might, steps forth to the rescue and the liberation of the old.

This was strong stuff, and the House of Commons, or at least its Conservative majority, once more listened to it in silence – a silence that could be interpreted as profound emotion, anxiety, or tacit dissent.

But Churchill knew what he was saying, and he knew how to prevail. At a time when nearly everyone else in the country was preoccupied with sheer survival – and when many a politician was probably wondering how Britain could, after a show of resistance, extricate herself relatively cheaply – Churchill was already planning a new wartime alliance with America and total victory. And if *this island* had to be sacrificed for the sake of that total victory, he told himself, so be it. It was Churchill's iron determination to win at absolutely any cost that made him 1940's man of destiny.

Churchill and Britain were not synonymous in 1940, although he always said so. *It was the nation and the race . . . that had the lion's heart,* he was generous enough to declare in later years. *I had the luck to be called upon to give the roar.*

But that was too modest. It is true that he had only a small personal share in Britain's remarkable defensive successes during 1940: the self-sacrificial rescue of the British Expeditionary Force from Dunkirk; victory in the air over Britain; and the Egyptian attack that routed the Italians' African army at the end of the year. He commented on these events rather than inspired them, and the British, with their backs to the wall, would probably have contrived to save their necks without him. Stolid, phlegmatic courage in adversity is a quality they have never lacked. But what they would have made of these successes without Churchill, and how things would have developed thereafter, is quite another matter. Even at heroic moments in her history, Britain has always had something of an eye to the main chance and contrived to terminate her wars in good time, hence the not entirely unmerited nickname 'perfidious Albion'. That this did not happen in 1940 was Churchill's handiwork.

There was also an unmistakable element of self-restraint in the singular fortitude and self-confidence with which the British defended themselves in 1940. At the end of May, when France was collapsing, hundreds of British fishermen and boat owners and yachtsmen braved the hail of bombs off Dunkirk to help bring the army home in their cockle-shells. In so doing, they demonstrated an islander's instinct as well as great personal courage. George VI, a far more typical Englishman than Churchill, confided at the time that he felt better now that Britain no longer had any allies to be handled

Second son of George V, George VI (1895–1952) became King of the United Kingdom (1936–52) following the abdication of his elder brother Edward VIII. After service in the Royal Navy in the First World War, he was created Duke of York in 1920. He reigned throughout the Second World War, residing in Buckingham Palace despite bomb damage. He was succeeded by his eldest daughter, Elizabeth II.

with kid gloves. Shortly afterwards, during one of the cautious, unofficial talks conducted here and there with neutrals, and even with German middlemen (Churchill stamped on these hard when they came to his attention), a British diplomat declared that the time for European guarantees was over, and that Britain must now think of herself.

He probably expressed the attitude of most Britons better than Churchill did after Dunkirk, when he promised to fight on even if *this island* were lost, or when, two weeks later, after the fall of France, he proclaimed: *We abate nothing of our just demands; not one jot or tittle do we recede. Czechs, Poles, Norwegians, Dutch, Belgians have joined their causes to our own. All these shall be restored . . . Hitler knows that he will have to break us in this island or lose the war.* Fundamentally, what Churchill was demanding in 1940, when the British were fighting for sheer survival, was Hitler's unconditional surrender.

According to Mao Zedong, the quintessence of all war is one's own preservation and the enemy's destruction. It could be said that 'Britain' and Churchill divided those war aims between them in 1940. 'Britain' was fighting for survival; the enemy's destruction was something with which she might, if necessary, have been prepared to dispense. But Churchill was firmly resolved to destroy the enemy, and he was ready, if the worst came to the worst, to sacrifice Britain's existence to that end. He did not know it, but he may have been laying the foundations of that profound, unspoken, subtle misunderstanding between himself and his country which in 1945, in the hour of his greatest outward triumph, led to his downfall.

What were the roots of his decision? Whence came the adamantine, doggedly destructive urge that turned the Churchill of 1940 into a legendary figure, a primeval warrior who fought the world bare-fisted while London burned around him?

Reading the hugely provocative, wholly uncompromising showers of abuse with which Churchill deluged victorious Hitler –

This wicked man, the repository and embodiment of many forms of soul-destroying hatred, this monstrous product of former wrongs and shame – we might for a moment believe that the radicalism of his youth had come to life in him once more, for those whose views he was expressing, and expressing in language that brought tears of emotion to their eyes, were the European and British leftists who had learned to hate Hitler like the devil incarnate. Churchill, for years a kind of junior devil in their eyes, became their hero in Britain and everywhere else.

It would be rash, however, to conclude that he had again rejoined the radical, progressive, left wing. The Churchill of the Second World War was very far from being a radical, as he clearly demonstrated during the subsequent course of the conflict, but he needed the Left because they alone shared his utter determination to destroy the enemy and emerge victorious. It was certainly not shared by the Conservatives, who, having until recently lauded Hitler and helped to build up his strength, still found it hard to grasp why their intended partnership with him had failed. Churchill wooed the Left with actions as well as words. Ernest Bevin, the great trade union boss who had jointly led the General Strike which Churchill had wanted to crush by unleashing civil war only 14 years earlier, was invited to join his Cabinet as Minister of Labour

Orphan and autodidact, Ernest Bevin (1881–1951) rose to the pinnacle of political power. A committed trade unionist he was one of the founders of the Transport and General Workers' Union (TGWU) and was its General Secretary from 1922 to 1940. A Labour MP from 1940, he served in Churchill's coalition and was Foreign Minister in the post-war Labour government.

and National Service – to all intents and purposes, Britain's wartime manpower dictator. Churchill played on every available instrument, left-wing anti-fascism included, but he himself was no left-wing anti-fascist even now.

So was he motivated by personal hatred of Hitler? The sense

WOOING THE LEFT

that he was fighting a personal duel undoubtedly played its part, and his abhorrence of the man was genuine enough. It was the abhorrence of a born grand seigneur for an upstart, and of a chivalrous and extremely humane person for a cruel and evil one. Although a born fighter, Churchill was humane to the point of soft-heartedness, rather in the way that many enthusiastic hunters of game are great animal lovers. He detested the infliction of cruelty on the weak and defeated, and that form of cruelty was, of course, one of Hitler's most salient characteristics. But to believe that purely personal feelings of hatred were Churchill's motive for waging a world war would be to underestimate him. Besides, it is remarkable how his hatred of Hitler waned in the course of the war. The tone in which he spoke of him in public changed. Abuse and unbridled vituperation were gradually replaced by mockery until in 1945, the year of victory, Churchill ceased to refer to Hitler at all. Hitler no longer interested him.

'That blatherer, that drunkard, Churchill, what has he achieved all his lifetime? That mendacious creature, that sluggard of the first order. Had this war not come, future centuries would have spoken of our age, of all of us, and also of myself, as the creators of great works of peace. But had this war not come, who would speak of Churchill? True – one day they will speak of him – as the destroyer of an empire which he, not we, has ruined. One of the most abominable glory-hunters in world history, incapable of a single creative action, capable only of destruction.' ADOLF HITLER

No, what motivated Churchill was neither anti-fascism nor personal hatred – nor even normal patriotism, or he would not have been so reckless in regard to Britain's interests and continuing existence. It was ambition, and ambition of a dual kind: that of the statesman and that of Churchill the man (one is almost tempted to say, of Churchill the artist).

The statesman's ambition on behalf of his country was probably, despite everything, his principal motive. That he risked his country's downfall, as we have shown, does not militate against this. Ambition and sacrifice are not mutually exclusive; indeed, they go together. Churchill was prepared to gamble with Britain's survival because he wished to spare her the humiliation of a compromise peace settlement at all costs.

For what were the facts? Britain had erected a stop sign in Hitler's path: after her experience of Munich and Prague, she had told him, in effect: 'If you attack Poland as well, we shall fight you to the death.' Contemptuously brushing this aside, Hitler had attacked and subjugated Poland, and Britain now had her work cut out to survive that fight to the death. If Britain had now, after defending herself with relative success, reached an accommodation with Hitler that preserved her own existence but confirmed his brutal conquest of Poland, the British politicians who had engineered such an accommodation (and there were several capable of doing so) would undoubtedly have represented this as a triumph of realistic statesmanship, and Britain, in her relief, might have accepted their view. It would nonetheless have been a terrible public humiliation.

On the other hand, if Britain now, in the direst danger, stood by her promise that an attack on Poland would cost Hitler his life – and if she eventually made good that promise – would not that redound to her credit more than any other chapter in her long history? And was it really so impossible? The one chance Churchill could see was called America.

If presented with a choice between supporting Britain or watching her go under, America would have to opt for the former course of action, because she could not afford to let Hitler become master of the Atlantic. If America supported Britain, however, she would sooner or later – with a little judicious prompting – have to enter the war fully on Britain's side. And the combined strength of America and the British Empire would, so Churchill believed, suffice for total victory.

But only just, perhaps. The war would certainly be a long one, because Britain herself was far from being fully armed and mobilized, and America had not even begun to rearm and mobilize. In addition to its horrors and suffering, however, didn't a long, jointly waged war present undreamed-of, triumphant, glorious prospects of convergence? If the defeat of Hitler helped to bring about something like a reunification of the English-speaking peoples, wouldn't the world lie at the feet of their combined might?

It can be demonstrated that Churchill clearly envisioned this process even in the darkest days of summer 1940. In August, when the Battle of Britain still hung in the balance and the country was threatened with an invasion it had little in the way of land forces to resist, Churchill told Parliament that *the British Empire and the United States will have to be somewhat mixed up together.* Then, abandoning the colloquial for the rhetorical, he spoke of the future unity of the English-speaking democracies, which would, *like the Mississippi . . . roll on in full flood, inexorable, irresistible, benignant, to broader lands and better days.* And, once again, he meant every word of it.

But the ambition of Churchill the statesman for his country must not blind us to the ambition of the man, the artist, the artist of war, for himself and his posthumous reputation.

Both were real and effective, and each would have been motive enough: the great, statesmanlike vision of a Britain that gloriously kept her word and enfolded America, after nearly two centuries of defection, in a new, more exalted form of union; and the burning personal ambition of an often rejected, almost defeated, almost despised old politician and practitioner of war who had now, *in extremis,* been entrusted with the conduct of a war so hopelessly mishandled as to be almost lost, and who was determined and confident of his ability to turn it into the greatest victory of all time, whatever the cost. So Churchill the statesman should not obscure Churchill the daemon, and vice versa. That they both attained their peak at this moment – the last moment for Britain, which was genuinely in dire straits, and also for Churchill himself, who at 65 was able to muster his flagging energies for a supreme personal effort – *that* was what made him a man of destiny and the year June 1940–June 1941 *his* year for evermore.

But what did he actually do during that year, and how, in concrete terms, did he turn 'the hinge of fate'? His contribution to Britain's defensive victories in 1940 should not be overstated, as we have said. His real achievements were of a different and unsung nature.

The crucial ones were four in number: the exclusion of all prominent politicians belonging to the appeasement school; the *coup d'état* – for so it should really be called – with which Churchill made himself a generalissimo; the ruthlessly effected mobilization of industry which, within six months, transformed Britain into a fortress bristling with weapons (and bankrupted her in the process); and Churchill's private correspondence with President Roosevelt, which bypassed all their diplomats and parliamentarians and forged the Anglo-American alliance.

Churchill disposed of the appeasers – and, with them, any possibility of a negotiated peace – with unwonted political dexterity.

Franklin Delano Roosevelt (1882–1945), 32nd President of the United States, was a former lawyer and suffered from polio. Governor of New York from 1929, he was elected President for the Democratic Party in 1933. After tackling the economic crisis of the Depression with his 'New Deal', he entered the Second World War in 1941 following the Japanese attack on Pearl Harbor. The only US President to be re-elected three times, he died on 12 April 1945, three weeks before the German surrender.

NO APPEASEMENT

He rejected vehement left-wing demands that the 'guilty men' be ostracized, magnanimously declaring that if the present sat in judgement on the past it would lose the future. All the leading figures of the appeasement period – who still represented the elite of the Conservative Party – were given senior posts that kept them fully occupied but shunted them into harmless sidings. One became Lord Chancellor, another President of the Board of Education charged with introducing radical reforms in the school system (which he conscientiously did, even at the height of the war), and another was packed off to Madrid as ambassador. The most important of all, Lord Halifax, a rival whom Churchill was initially compelled to retain as Secretary of State for Foreign Affairs, took over the British embassy in Washington at the end of the year. Although he was loaded down with honours and nominally retained his seat in the War Cabinet, this got him out of the way. When Chamberlain resigned the leadership of the Conservative Party shortly before his death, Churchill prevailed on the reluctant Conservatives to adopt him as Chamberlain's successor; as things stood in the autumn of 1940, they had no choice. The party that had never liked him, the only one still capable of wrecking his policy, was now firmly in his grasp. He would not release his hold on it for another 15 years.

Churchill was assiduous in attending Parliament. As for his War Cabinet, which he quite conventionally recruited from the leading politicians of all parties, he always made a point of modestly representing it as the supreme authority and decision-making body. But he also, by a stroke of genius, appointed himself Minister of Defence, an entirely new post whose powers he refrained from defining. In reality, this made him a generalissimo and demoted the three service ministers to the status of mere auxiliaries and administrators. As Minister of Defence he tacitly presided over the heads of all the services, thus becoming supreme commander and chief of all the chiefs of staff; and Prime Minister Churchill protected Generalissimo Churchill from all attempts at political interference.

As Prime Minister, Churchill ruled, on the whole, with a light hand; as generalissimo, with a rod of iron. In accordance with his well-known views on 'old fogeys', he instituted a ruthless clearance among the British military. The Chief of the Imperial General Staff had to go at once, the Chief of Air Staff a few months later. As for how many generals Churchill fired in the course of the war, they defy enumeration.

Generalissimo Churchill was not infallible. He made the mistake typical of all amateur strategists (and despite his young days in the army he was, when all is said and done, an amateur strategist like Stalin and Hitler): he demanded too much of his armed forces. This worked with the navy and air force – repeatedly presented with almost unachievable tasks, they fought throughout the war with professional stoicism and courage – but Churchill was a questionable warlord where Britain's conscript army of almost five million was concerned. Its morale suffered from constant overstrain, and the middle of the war brought episodes like the surrender, almost without a fight, of Singapore and Tobruk. It took the special talents of Field Marshal Montgomery – whose popularity with the army far exceeded Churchill's in the closing stages of the war – to nurse the conscript army's morale back to health and spur it into a respectable final gallop.

Field Marshal Bernard Montgomery 'Monty' (1887–1976) rose to prominence in the Second World War. He commanded a division at Dunkirk before becoming Commander of the 8th Army in North Africa in 1942, then Commander of Allied land forces for the D-Day landings. A vain and controversial figure, he squabbled with the Americans and was defeated at Arnhem. He became Chief of the Imperial General Staff after the war.

But Generalissimo Churchill cannot be denied the credit for one great achievement: he forged the three armed services, which had pursued their own jealous existence throughout the First World

Churchill and Field Marshal Montgomery on a tour of troops gathering for the 'D Day' invasion of France

War and early in the Second, into an effective totality. Under his leadership there were no more disastrous failures of army-navy co-operation like the Dardanelles and Norway, and it was he who made possible the ever greater feats of organization that facilitated the large-scale amphibious landings in North Africa, Sicily, Italy, and Normandy. Despite his many hare-brained acts and military flights of fancy, this was an achievement which does, after all, rank him among the great military leaders of all time.

Churchill's third achievement was total mobilization, a policy he pursued almost precipitately and with the utmost ruthlessness. At Easter 1940, Britain's beaches had still been crowded with holiday-makers, the roads leading to the sea jammed with cars. Her luxury hotels still boasted uniformed porters, her industrial cities housed a million unemployed. Critics of the Chamberlain Cabinet's financial policy during the first winter of the conflict scathingly opined that its purpose seemed to be to render Britain capable of paying Germany reparations after losing the war. Churchill promptly put a stop to this. His first parliamentary bill, which was unanimously passed on 22 May, placed every person and all property in Britain unreservedly at the Government's disposal for military purposes. Six months later there were no unemployed, the beaches had become army training areas, and civil servants occupied the requisitioned hotels. The factories were turning out weapons and war materials 24 hours a day, exports had almost dried up, and the country's last foreign exchange reserves were being expended on arms purchases. By the end of 1940, Britain's export trade was bankrupt and her balance of payments wrecked – precisely what Chamberlain had always dreaded and what Britain was to labour under for many years to come. On the other hand, having been almost defenceless after Dunkirk, she could now muster 29 almost fully armed divisions, and her ports and airfields teemed with more

Churchill and Attlee inspect the new Lancaster bomber

BRITAIN BANKRUPT

warships and many more warplanes than she had possessed before the costly naval and air battles of the foregoing months.

What was more, Churchill knew how to make a weapon of war even out of the bankruptcy he had deliberately accepted. The Americans could evade the issue no longer. They would either have to continue supplying Britain on credit, thereby publicly siding with her, or write off all they had supplied hitherto, let Britain go under, and make Hitler master of the Atlantic. Having already submitted them to the moral pressure of London in the Blitz, Churchill finally coerced them with the bankruptcy weapon.

For that was Churchill's fourth and most difficult achievement: the ensnaring and involvement of the United States in Britain's war, a goal he tirelessly pursued by every available means from ardent courtship to cold-blooded blackmail. He maintained a continuous private correspondence with President Roosevelt to which he devoted at least as much care as to the drafting of his major speeches. Being an enemy of the European dictators for reasons of his own, Roosevelt was not averse to joining a European crusade. But 1940 was a presidential election year, and he had to proceed with extreme caution. His country's mood was anything but warlike and favourable to intervention. Not only was America completely disarmed, but, even if she began to rearm, was it still worth investing war capital in the bankrupt British concern? Wasn't Britain's war lost beyond redemption? The then US ambassador in London, Joseph Kennedy (father of the president-to-be) said so day after day in the reports he sent home.

Churchill seized on this. His task was difficult to the point of impossibility. On the one hand he had to convince Roosevelt that Britain was far from defeated; on the other, that she would collapse without urgently needed assistance. On the one hand he had to reassure Roosevelt that the British Empire would never surrender, even if *this island* were lost; on the other, he could not afford to lull him into the belief that, if the worst happened, America could become *heir to the Empire minus Britain*. His principal means of pressure was to threaten Roosevelt with the consequences of a hypothetical British surrender (a surrender negotiated by another government; he, Churchill, would never give in – he once told the Cabinet that he would sooner choke on his own blood on the doorstep of 10 Downing Street). The price his successor would have to pay for German leniency towards a defeated Britain consisted, quite clearly, in the British fleet. And if Hitler acquired the British fleet in addition to the French, Italian, and German, his domination of the Atlantic would extend to America's eastern seaboard. Churchill never tired of impressing this on Roosevelt. He also appealed to America's conscience. His classic tribute to the Battle of Britain fighter pilots in August 1940 – *Never in the field of human conflict was so much owed by so many to so few* – was directed mainly at the United States.

Until Britain's bankruptcy became obvious, the results of all Churchill's efforts were pathetically small and painfully slow in

Churchill on the deck of the battleship *Prince of Wales* on his return from the USA 1941

coming. Britain had to go bankrupt in order to bring about the decisive turning point, a public commitment on America's part to supply the British with war material gratis by means of a clever subterfuge: the American 'Lend-Lease' Act in March 1941, or the fiction that Britain was only 'borrowing' and 'leasing' American arms and munitions.

Lend-Lease – the system by which the United States was able to supply Britain, France, and the USSR during the Second World War without formally breaking her neutrality – began in spring 1941. With the issue of repayment or return deferred to the end of hostilities, Lend-Lease was extended following the American entry into the war in December 1941. By its termination in 1945, Lend-Lease had supplied $43 billion of military and industrial aid.

Churchill may have hoped that such an open breach of neutrality would goad Hitler into declaring war on the United States and thereby relieve him of all his worries, but nothing came of it at first. Hitler, who had resolved on war with Russia, temporarily ignored America's hostile acts. The whole of 1941 went by in this way, although Roosevelt, who had since won another four years in office, kept provoking Hitler with pinpricks and edged closer, step by step, to open participation in the war.

It is impossible here to trace all the twists and turns, hopes and disappointments, of this long and complicated story. It attained a final, almost unbearable pitch of suspense in the late autumn of 1941, when it became clear that Japan, too, was poised to attack. 'When the storm wind blows in the west, the leaves fall in the east,' the Japanese Foreign Minister had floridly declared, and the Japanese were preparing to gather up the fallen leaves. But which leaves? What if they confined themselves to acquiring the British, French, and Dutch possessions in the Far East and prudently left the United States unscathed? Would the Americans regard this as an act of war? Roosevelt, still unsure if he could take the plunge, said nothing. And again, even if Japan attacked America too, would America focus all her efforts on Japan and forget about

Britain's European war? There was more than one answer to these tormenting questions. If the answer turned out to be the wrong one, everything Churchill had so patiently planned and prepared for in growing collusion with Roosevelt would have been in vain: his whole strategic concept would be knocked on the head, and he himself could do nothing about it. He was once more in the hands of blind fate. But hadn't destiny, which had so often duped and toyed with him, proved ultimately to be his faithful ally? Or was it capable of duping him yet again and still more cruelly?

The Sino-Japanese War (1937–45) was but the final stage in a prolonged period of Japanese aggression towards China, which began with the occupation of Manchuria in 1931. It was also the true beginning of the Second World War. When Japan attacked the United States in 1941, the Sino-Japanese War became part of a much wider conflagration.

Pearl Harbor and Hitler's declaration of war on the United States on 11 December 1941 delivered Churchill from the torment of those weeks. They came as an unparalleled relief and took an immense weight off his mind. While Britain was groaning under the impact of the bad news from the Far East, Churchill resembled a man long accustomed to living under sentence of death who suddenly hears that he is to go free. Pearl Harbor had half released him; Hitler's declaration of war on the United States completed the process.

Pearl Harbor was the US naval base on Oahu, Hawaii, bombed by the Japanese in a surprise attack on 7 December 1941. Nineteen US ships were lost and some 2,000 servicemen killed. As a result the US entered the Second World War.

There are several accounts of his reaction to the news, and all are reminiscent of a dam bursting. The fierce old warrior yielded to a fit of exultant, exuberant jubilation that transformed him into a boy once more. *Now we've done it!* he exclaimed again and again. *Now we've won the war!* No one actually says so, but all these accounts convey the impression that Winston Churchill got drunk that night.

Triumph and Tragedy · 1942–1945

Where Churchill himself was concerned, the war fell into three clearly defined phases. The first lasted from May 1940 to December 1941. That was when danger threatened – the deadly, immediate danger presented by Hitler alone. He came through that perilous phase with flying colours.

Hitler ceased to be a serious threat after December 1941. From December 1941 until November 1942, an intermediate period during which defeat no longer loomed but victory was not yet in sight, the threat to Churchill emanated from political circles at home. There was a sudden resurgence of criticism and opposition from forces intent on bringing him down. He disposed of that danger, and from late 1942 until the end of the war he enjoyed a period of calm – deceptive calm, as it turned out.

During this third phase, however, his allies became his real opponents: not only Stalin but, from the end of 1943, Roosevelt as well. Churchill lost to them. Final victory over Hitler, who had ceased to be important by May 1945, carried a bitter taste because it sealed his defeat by Stalin and Roosevelt.

And then, while he was desperately and indomitably searching for ways of snatching victory from that defeat, his success on the home front in 1942 turned out to be a pyrrhic victory: in July 1945 he lost the general election and was stripped of power.

What was it that had suddenly rendered the home front danger-ous to him in 1942? From a superficial (though not necessarily

Churchill seated with military leaders in Algiers

mistaken) point of view, simply the fact that 1942 was a year in which Britain sustained some grave military reverses.

For all their extreme and unremitting danger, the years 1940 and 1941 had brought many notable defensive successes. (The failure of an occasional lunge like the ill-starred Greek expedition was deemed to be acceptable.) After 1942 came an almost unbroken succession of victories, but during that year everything that could go wrong did go wrong. The Japanese overran Malaya and Burma and threatened India. The German Field Marshal Rommel defeated the Army of the Nile and pushed deep into Egypt. The 'impregnable' fortress of Singapore abjectly surrendered with the loss of 100,000 men. Tobruk, the isolated desert stronghold that had held out for many months the year before, was captured at the first attempt in a single day. The overstretched Royal Navy suffered

Field Marshal Erwin Rommel (1891–1944) was one of the outstanding military tacticians of the Second World War. After service in the First World War, he taught at the Dresden Military Academy before commanding Hitler's headquarters. He achieved major successes as commander of the German 'Afrika Korps', but was defeated by the British 8th Army. Returning to Germany in 1944, he was implicated in a plot to kill Hitler and committed suicide.

ROMMEL

terrible losses in the Pacific, the Indian Ocean, the Mediterranean, and while escorting Arctic convoys to Russia. Sinkings of merchantmen by U-boats steadily increased. An experimental invasion at Dieppe proved a disastrous failure. The Indians became refractory, and the British imprisoned Gandhi and Nehru for the last time.

Jawaharlal 'Pandit' Nehru (1889–1964) was a follower of Gandhi and President of the Indian National Congress. After Indian independence in 1947, he was India's first Prime Minister and Minister of External Affairs. He pursued policies of domestic industrialization and neutrality during the Cold War.

Old memories revived – memories of Churchill the reactionary, who had always been wrong in pre-Hitler days. First and foremost, however, he was blamed for the sudden, continuous series of defeats on land and sea. He had been engaged because he knew something about war, but it was clear that he didn't know as much about it as he thought. Things were steadily getting worse instead of better.

In July a motion of no confidence was proposed in Parliament. It was voted down, but the crisis smouldered on. In September a cabinet crisis loomed, and with it the sudden appearance of a rival for the premiership: Sir Stafford Cripps, as much of an outsider on the Left as Churchill had been on the Right. Cripps would never have stood a chance of becoming Prime Minister in peacetime, but anything was possible in wartime and under an all-party coalition. Being Churchill's antitype, he exerted a sudden fascination exactly proportionate to the growing extent of people's disappointment with Churchill. He was an ascetic, a coldly brilliant intellectual, a blend of puritanism and radicalism, undoubtedly a great

A lawyer and Labour politician, Stafford Cripps (1889–1952) was a militant socialist frequently at odds with his party. Sent as ambassador to Moscow in 1940, he did much to foster Anglo-Russian accord, and returned to join the War Cabinet in 1942. A brilliant but cold and austere man, he became a critic of Churchill's direction of the war. He was appointed Chancellor of the Exchequer in 1947.

man in his thin-lipped, razor-sharp way, but handicapped by a trace of vegetarian insipidity.

In September he submitted his resignation from the Cabinet in terms that clearly set him up as a rival for the premiership. Churchill managed to persuade him to defer his resignation until the large-scale operations impending in North Africa were under way. These brought a turning point in the war, saved Churchill, and put paid to Cripps. Churchill demoted him to Minister of Aircraft Production, and he never again presented a threat.

Such episodes are revealing, and there is a certain automatic justice about their outcome. Had Cripps been the Robespierre many thought him, he would not have granted a postponement; he would have waged a hard-fought duel just when Churchill was at his weakest. It is not beyond the bounds of possibility that Churchill would have stepped down in October 1942 just as Asquith did in December 1916, and that Cripps would have become the Lloyd George of the Second World War.

Would that have been a misfortune – other than from Churchill's point of view? Cripps was no generalissimo and no war hero like him, he was a pure politician. But the foundations of final victory had been laid by the autumn of 1942 (despite all the defeats of that year, which deeply shocked the country, but which Churchill, from a broader strategic aspect, saw as the episodes they were); and Cripps the politician might possibly have fitted into the landscape of the second half of the war better than Churchill.

Sir Stafford Cripps and Mahatma Gandhi at Birla Park in Delhi in 1942

What had also occasioned the crisis in 1942, apart from underlying disquiet at that year's military setbacks, were deeper, temporarily unarticulated worries about Churchill's general policy. There was a widespread sense that he was covertly playing too big and audacious a game, a feeling more justified than temporary disappointment at his conduct of the war. Although that feeling was allayed by the victories of the ensuing two and a half years, it remained latent until July 1945, when it vented itself in the sudden explosion that swept Churchill from office.

Britain was undoubtedly the smallest and weakest partner in the grand alliance which Churchill and Hitler, in the almost mystical collaboration that characterized their relationship from first to last, had brought about in 1941. Her logical policy would then have been to make herself useful as a link for as long as necessary, husband her strength as much as possible, and, when the time came, see to it that the inevitable victory of her two colossal allies was not so complete as to prevent the defeated countries from being factors in the international balance of power.

Churchill probably grasped this, but he also discerned a more glorious possibility: a way of enabling Britain, although the smallest partner, to dominate and control the grand coalition. He believed that he could make the tail wag the dog, as it were. It was not that he wanted to render victory incomplete or deliberately vitiate it. He did not aspire to personify both Marlborough *and* his adversary, Bolingbroke, who had gone behind the then generalissimo's back and paved the way for an advantageous but rather discreditable separate peace with Louis XIV; that would have gone against the grain. He wanted not only to destroy Hitler but, at the same time, to shut out Stalin and harness Roosevelt to Britain so tightly that the United States would never be able to detach itself again.

For that he needed the war to follow a course that would physically exclude Russia from Europe. This entailed that the major

Anglo-American offensive should be directed at Eastern, not Western, Europe. The thrust that broke Germany's back must simultaneously drive a steel wedge between Europe and the Soviet Union. And this meant, in turn, that it must be conducted from the south, not the west; based on North Africa, not the British Isles; launched across the Mediterranean, not the Channel; and aimed in the direction, not of Paris, Cologne and the Ruhr, but of Trieste, Vienna, and Prague, whereafter it would proceed to Berlin or even Warsaw.

If this plan succeeded, the war's end would see the combined armies of Britain and the United States in sole occupation and control of Europe. The Soviet Union would remain within its borders. France would never again become a theatre of war; liberated and a trifle ashamed, she would rise again unscathed. As for the Anglo-American partnership that would give liberated and occupied Europe its new appearance, Churchill believed he could dominate it.

On an inspection of several bomb-damaged cities, Churchill visits Manchester in 1941

US soldier and politician, George Marshall (1880–1959) served as Chief of Staff (1939–45) and was appointed Secretary of State in 1947. He put his name to the Marshall Plan for the post-war reconstruction of Europe, which greatly assisted the material and economic revival of Western Europe. He was awarded the Nobel Peace Prize in 1953.

A dazzling vision, but how to realize it? How to implement such a strategy? Churchill could never disclose its political objective, least of all to the Russians, but not to the Americans either. Besides, every strategic argument militated against it. To make a giant detour via North Africa instead of taking the direct route via France would naturally be time-wasting and debilitating – any student of war could see that, and the American generals, with Marshall and Eisenhower at their head, never tired of pointing this out.

US soldier and politician Dwight Eisenhower (1890–1969) was supreme commander of the Allied Expeditionary Force in the 1944 invasion of Europe. He was made supreme commander of NATO forces in Europe in 1950 and was elected US President as a Republican in 1952. He was re-elected in 1956 for a second term.

But Churchill held a trump card: the Americans were two years behind the British, not only in military preparedness but in the actual conduct of war. If they did not want to wait until they could wage their own war in two or three years' time – and America is an impatient country – they had no choice but to join in Britain's war as it stood and reinforce her with their initially slender but gradually increasing military resources. And Britain was already committed in North Africa.

Neither Roosevelt nor Stalin had any interest in backing Churchill's southern strategy and its ulterior political motives – in fact Stalin had every reason, and made every effort, to thwart it. However, Churchill initially succeeded in imposing his strategy on the others. What is more, he did so in the summer of 1942, when blows were raining down on him from all sides and the ground at home was giving way beneath him.

Churchill and his emblematic V for Victory sign that became his trademark during the Second World War

Churchill in 1942 was the man of destiny no longer. He eventually lost the over-audacious game he embarked on at that time, and, not that he knew it, his days as a genuine maker of world history were already over. But anyone wishing to see him at the very height of his personal dynamism and splendour would do well to take a look at him in 1942. He seemed to be 20 men that summer. He defended himself in Parliament, neutralized Cripps, planned campaigns with his chiefs of staff, dealt with American envoys, flew to Egypt and fired or appointed generals, flew to Washington and worked on Roosevelt, flew to Moscow and did battle with Stalin. Never had he more closely resembled the bulldog that never lets go, burying its teeth ever deeper the harder it is beaten. And by the end of that year he had everything just as he wanted it – for the moment: Hitler and Stalin locked in combat in the depths of Russia, Rommel defeated and the Mediterranean prised open, America deployed in North Africa at Britain's side. All was in readiness for next year's leap across the Mediterranean. At the turn of 1942–3 Churchill seemed to hold the world in his fist.

A year later his strategy – and consequently his policy – lay in ruins. He had assumed that it was almost impossible to reverse a strategic initiative in wartime; that the train, once on a certain track, would have to continue in the same direction. While actively committing the Americans to his Mediterranean strategy, he had always paid lip service – sometime, later, eventually – to an invasion from the west. He had not counted on their taking him at his word. He had not thought it possible that they could bring themselves to nullify the massive Mediterranean campaign into which he had manoeuvred them, and to which they had initially contributed all they possessed, by brutally winding it down, reducing it to a useless torso, redirecting all their resources, accepting six months' loss of time, and starting again from scratch with quite another orientation. But that is precisely what they did.

The dog had grown tired of being wagged by its tail. By late 1943, after two years' rearmament and mobilization, the Americans were ready, able, and determined to wage a war of their own. They were no longer dependent on assisting the British. At the Teheran Conference at the end of November 1943, Roosevelt and Stalin joined forces against Churchill, who had no choice but to grit his teeth and abandon his strategic and political grand design of the previous year.

The decision taken at Teheran, which was put into effect in the summer of 1944 and shaped the post-war history of Europe, liquidated Churchill's southern strategy and replaced it with the invasion of France. Not only strategic but eminently political

The first tripartite inter-Allied conference of the Second World War, Teheran (November–December 1943) was attended by Stalin, Roosevelt, and Churchill. It dealt with issues such as the planned Allied landings in France, the Soviet offensive against Germany, and post-war inter-national organizations. The failure to agree on the future government of Poland foreshadowed the start of the Cold War.

as well, it was a decision that failed to exclude Russia from Europe and led to an East-West confrontation in the heart of that continent. This put paid to Churchill's vision of a Europe in his own image – a conservative Europe restored under American auspices – and ensured that post-war Europe would be either 'left-wing', 'democratic', and more or less socialist, or divided.

Although the participants in the Teheran Conference doubtless realized all this, it was not explicitly stated. The arguments employed were exclusively strategic, and the truth was that Churchill's strategic position had been badly weakened during 1943.

Like everyone else, he had made two miscalculations: he overestimated the effects of air power and underestimated the Soviet Union. He believed that the great bombing offensive initiated in 1943 would wear down Germany's home front and render her ripe for surrender, and that the Russians, despite their series of winter successes, would only just survive and be hard put to it to defend Leningrad, Moscow, and Stalingrad during the summer campaigns. The German armies deep inside Russia, and Germany herself in a state of chaos and dissolution: that was the scenario to which Churchill's strategy was tailored. In such circumstances, the Mediterranean countries would fall into the Allied invaders' arms with a sigh of relief (as Italy actually tried to do in the summer of 1943), and the victorious British and Americans would suddenly appear in undefended Saxony and Silesia. Such was Churchill's plan, but it did not, as we know, work out.

In fact, the bombing campaign proved as blunt an intimidatory weapon in Germany as it had previously done in Britain. The home front stood firm and German war production continued full blast. On the other hand, the combat effectiveness and fighting spirit of German forces on the Eastern Front were no longer what they had been before Stalingrad. Now in the ascendant, both materially and morally, the Russians had driven the Germans back throughout 1943 and were almost at the borders of Romania and Poland. Meanwhile, the Western Allies' armies were still bogged down outside Cassino, well to the south of Rome. If the pattern of 1943 were repeated, the Russians would be in Warsaw, Berlin, and possibly on the Rhine while the Western Allies were still agonizing south of the Alps. This being so, Churchill was almost bereft of arguments in the strategic debate conducted at Teheran.

Should he have argued his case politically with Roosevelt (he could not, of course, have done so with Stalin)? Should he have put his cards on the table and painted an ominous picture of the Russian threat? It is doubtful if he would have succeeded. Quite apart from the fact that it was now too late to exclude Russia from Europe militarily, and that it was quite possible to argue that sharing Europe with the Russians was the only alternative to abandoning it to them altogether, Roosevelt believed in the possibility of

US-Soviet co-operation in a 'left-wing' Europe. It is unlikely that he would have been weaned from that belief by Churchill the conservative romantic.

Not even Churchill was capable of attempting such a thing. For all his eloquence, he suffered from a lifelong absence of the talent that constituted Lloyd George's greatest strength: the gift of seductive persuasion – of 'talking people round' – that presupposes a capacity and liking for empathy, for feeling one's way into the minds of others. Lloyd George, coincidentally but significantly a great ladies' man, possessed that ability to an exceptional degree; Churchill the warrior and egocentric did not. Unlike Lloyd George or Bismarck, both of whom had dictated wartime policy regardless of strategy and over the heads of their strategists, thereby incurring constant friction with their military commanders, Churchill instinctively made policy by means of strategy. He preferred to assume the generalissimo's role himself and adduce his political arguments in the form of fleet and troop movements. This was his innate style. He could not do otherwise – hence the misconception of him entertained by those who seek to infer his ideas from his words as opposed to his actions. For three years he had successfully pursued a policy on the grandest scale by strategic means. Now that this instrument of policy had failed him, he was literally defenceless.

For Churchill, the Teheran Conference was not only the turning point of the war but a watershed in his life. His sixty-ninth birthday occurred halfway through the conference. Till then the immense physical and mental strain to which the war had subjected him so late in life had been scarcely noticeable. He still had the face of a rosy-cheeked baby, albeit a stern-looking baby with a jutting chin; his capacity for work and concentration, his self-control, power of decision, and stamina still verged on the miraculous. But suddenly, in the middle of the conference, he aged from hour to hour,

OUTMANOEUVRED

becoming long-winded, forgetful, erratic. During intervals in the talks he spoke grimly of the war the Western Allies were letting themselves in for – a future war with the Soviet Union. *There might be a more bloody war. I shall not be there. I shall be asleep. I want to sleep for billions of years.* It did not sound statesmanlike; prophetic, perhaps, but in a rather senile way.

Intermittently, however, he pulled himself together and played the good loser, only to renew his attempt to wangle concessions out of the victors with all too obvious guile. Very well, he said, the invasion in the west was resolved upon. He promised that it would take place by 1 May – or thereabouts. But should they squander the intervening six months in idleness? What if he managed to persuade Turkey to enter the war? Why not first launch a Balkan campaign – as an interlude, just to fill in the time? Roosevelt and Stalin exchanged meaningful looks and graciously allowed old Winston to ride his hobby horse. Let him try to inveigle Turkey into entering the war, they thought. They banked on the probability that the wary Turks would not be persuaded, and they were right.

At Carthage, where he intended to confer with Eisenhower on the way back from Teheran, Churchill was laid low by a severe bout of pneumonia – a stress-induced ailment if ever there was one – and hovered between life and death for several days. Having overcome this crisis with the aid of powerful antibiotics, he promptly laid plans for another 'interlude': a landing near Rome designed to set the stalled Italian campaign in motion. Would the Americans really have the heart to denude that front just when it was forging ahead once more? But the landing at Anzio, too, became bogged down, and it was a dejected Churchill who returned to London in the depths of winter 1944.

His behaviour after the Teheran Conference became some-what incoherent and unpredictable, somewhat 'hand-to-mouth'. He was still – or once more – brimming with energy and ideas, still

Churchill and Lt General Anderson leave the old Roman theatre at Carthage after addressing British troops in North Africa

vigorous and eloquent, still capable of great decisions and actions, but his decisions tended to be precipitate and his actions off-the-cuff. They were no longer based on a grand design. That had been wrecked, and its disappointed author was no longer quite the man he had been three years earlier. He was still the same person, but older, more irascible, and less self-controlled.

He had always been imperious, but not even anger had robbed him of his dignity. The Churchill of 1944 and 1945 often had undignified tantrums. Although still capable of magnanimous gestures and great moments, he now displayed an unexpectedly quarrelsome, petulant side.

This was when there also emerged the characteristics typical of Churchill's old age: a tendency toward lax inconsistency and mutually contradictory, self-negating gestures and actions. He had

AN OLD MAN

always been capable of entertaining many different ideas and emotions at once. That was what had endowed his psyche with such a wealth of dynamism, with the sparkling vitality, changeability, and unpredictability that had always distinguished him. Up to now, however, he had also possessed the inward power of decision that eventually, by engaging in a process of synthesis or exclusion, instilled order and clarity. That faculty was on the wane. There was something fragmentary and insufficiently well-weighed about Churchill's speeches and actions in old age: he took gigantic strides, only to halt halfway there. All this began in 1944.

At first, however, he enthusiastically immersed himself in military preparations for the great invasion he had not wanted. It was like a form of self-anaesthesia: if the politician had failed, the strategist at least wanted his due. Churchill the generalissimo had never been more restless or active – never happier, one might almost say. He spent the first five months of 1944 up to his eyes in invasion

Churchill, Lt General Dempsey and Field Marshal Montgomery viewing the ruins of Caen after the D-Day invasion

plans, attended to all the details, and was dissuaded only with the utmost difficulty from landing in France with the forward elements (George VI eventually threatened that, if Churchill insisted on going, he would come too). He yearned for the victory whose prisoner he had become; there was nothing else he could do.

Churchill and the Chiefs of Staff observing enemy aircraft above Normandy after the D-Day and the Allied invasion of France

Or might there have been? When victory beckoned in earlier wars of alliance, Britain had not balked at bringing the enemy back into the political game, whether indirectly, as in the war against Louis XIV, or directly, as in the war against Napoleon, when British diplomats put out feelers to Talleyrand and the Bourbons. Negotiating with Hitler was out of the question, admittedly; the man who had strewn the whole of Europe with human abattoirs was not only beyond the pale but totally opposed to negotiation. But what of the members of the German resistance, who had just made a belated and despairing sign of life on 20 July? From Churchill's point of view, wouldn't they have been the natural, almost heaven-sent negotiating partner?

The attempted assassination of Hitler on 20 July 1944 was the culmination of the German anti-Nazi resistance movement. Following the bomb attack on Hitler's headquarters, in which the Führer was only slightly wounded, the plot was uncovered by the Gestapo. The conspirators were rounded up and executed.

Didn't they fundamentally aspire to what he himself wanted – and what Stalin and Roosevelt most definitely did not want: the restoration of a conservative Europe?

Although this may with hindsight appear to have been a missed opportunity, it never really existed. Not only had the German resistance shown itself to be weak, irresolute and unreliable during the first winter of the war, when Chamberlain had genuinely maintained contact with it, and not only did the abortive putsch of 20 July fail to make an encouraging impression, but Churchill himself was not the man to endanger or impair victory – total victory, it now seemed almost certain – by engaging in such reckless dealings. He was a warrior first and a politician second. He wanted victory, and he wanted it to entail the victory of his political ideas. If that was impossible, however, he wanted victory anyway and under all circumstances. Magnanimity in victory and reconciliation thereafter, yes, but forgo victory? No, a thousand times no. He was and remained a descendant of Marlborough. He could not extend even literary forgiveness to the latter's rival, Bolingbroke, who had debased his victory for the sake of a more favourable peace settlement.

Churchill, Roosevelt and Stalin in the grounds of the Livadia Palace in the Crimea during the Yalta Conference July 1945

Churchill got his victory, and it cannot be said that he failed to relish it. There were great and wonderful moments, for instance his reunion with liberated Paris, but he remained the captive of his victory, chafing like a lion rubbing itself raw against the bars of its cage. His policy in the last nine months of the war was a series of improvisations, of restless comings and goings. In August 1944 he flew to Italy full of desperate (and ill-considered) plans for rendering a breakthrough to Trieste and Vienna feasible after all. To no avail, because the Italian front had been ruthlessly weakened and denuded in favour of the French campaign. Then he had a sudden idea. If Roosevelt could negotiate hard with Stalin, face to face, great power to great power, why shouldn't he do likewise? In October he flew to Moscow and drove a hard, cynical bargain with Stalin: Romania for you, Greece for me, Poland extended westwards – an arrangement demonstrated with the aid of three matches. What followed was his ugliest episode, accompanied by scenes better forgotten. When Mikolajczyk, the Polish premier, refused to be sold down the river, Churchill literally threatened him with his fist; and, when liberated Athens rose against the conservative government installed by its British liberators, he gave orders that it should be treated like a captured city. Stalin looked on without comment, and Churchill declared in the House of Commons that no government had ever kept its word more faithfully than that of the Soviet Union. In the spring of 1945, however, when the Anglo-American armies were presented with an unexpected chance to reach Berlin and the Oder ahead of the Russians, he did his utmost to persuade General Eisenhower and President Truman to seize that unlooked-for opportunity – even though it would not have been fully consistent with the previous three-power agreements on the zones of occupation into which Germany was to be divided. Similarly, if Churchill had had his way, the Western Allies would never have withdrawn to the agreed demarcation

Harry S Truman (1884–1972), the 33rd President of the United States, became Vice-President to Roosevelt in 1944, and succeeded upon the latter's death in April 1945. After the Second World War he instituted a policy of 'containment' of Communism, through the Marshall Plan, the Truman Doctrine, and NATO. He established the CIA and ordered the Berlin Airlift of 1948–9. He left office in 1953.

line from Saxony, Thuringia, and Mecklenburg. Russia had become the enemy once more.

Did he seriously contemplate redirecting the war against Russia in the early summer of 1945? He has been credited with such an intention, and he himself must have believed, at least in retrospect, that he entertained it. At all events, he later claimed to have given orders in May 1945 that captured German weapons should be carefully collected and maintained so that, if need be, they could be quickly reissued to German prisoners of war. The telegram to this effect has never been

Churchill and President Truman meet for the first time at the Potsdam Conference, 1945

found – it was probably never sent – but Churchill must have had such a directive in mind, or his memory would not have deluded him into believing that he had actually issued it.

What is certain is that he re-adopted a tough line against Russia in the summer of 1945, and that this realigned him with powerful currents of opinion in the United States. Roosevelt was dead. At the same time, Germany had scarcely surrendered when America embarked on full demobilization. What was brewing was not a war but the unproductive squabble that later became known as the Cold War.

The Cold War: the tensions and latent hostilities that characterized the relationship between the USSR and the major Western powers, especially the United States, following the Second World War. Intensified by the nuclear arms race, the Cold War entered a process of détente in the 1960s with a series of arms reduction and control programmes. The conflict formally ended with the East European revolutions of 1989 and the collapse of the Soviet Union in 1991.

Churchill had no chance to take an active part in it. The British coalition government disintegrated in May 1945. In July the Conservatives, with Churchill at their head, lost the general election. In spite of him? Because of him? Whatever the truth, Churchill had fallen once more.

At 70, he seemed to have reached the end of the road.

The Final Struggle · 1945–1965

When Churchill was voted out of office in July 1945, his wife remarked that it might be a blessing in disguise. *It may well be a blessing in disguise,* he retorted. *At the moment it seems quite effectively disguised.*

Most people would have agreed with his wife. By almost coinciding with the moment of victory, Churchill's fall provided him with a glorious exit. The war was over. Britain had come through it with flying colours, her enemies were destroyed, and no one could deny that this was largely to Churchill's credit. He knew,

Churchill with King George VI and Queen Elizabeth on the balcony of Buckingham Palace at the end of the War in Europe in May 1945

of course, that victory would pose as many problems as it solved, but he was temporarily alone in that realization. His country had yet to discover the truth. Anyone but Churchill might have been glad not to be held responsible for the disenchantment and disappointment to come.

Besides, he was 70 now, and the last five years had counted double. Physically, the Churchill of 1945 was no longer the Churchill of 1940. He had aged. Utterly exhausted and a prey to insomnia, he was irritable, nervous, and rather acerbic. The exhaustion he could possibly overcome, but there was no escaping old age. Anyway, wasn't his work already done? Hadn't he gloriously accomplished the providential task for which he had waited all his life?

Everything was in favour of calling it a day. Honours were his in plenty. People waved and cheered him wherever he showed his face, not only in Britain but in the South of France, where he took a holiday for the first time in six years, and even, to his bewilderment, in occupied Berlin. A dukedom would have been his for the

Crowds cheering Churchill in Liverpool

A HERO

asking. British and American cities and universities competed for the privilege of bestowing honorary citizenship and honorary doctorates upon him. In old age he even became, without any effort on his part, a very wealthy man: all his books had suddenly become international bestsellers.

One more literary work remained to be added: everyone was awaiting his personal account of the Second World War. Wouldn't that be occupation enough for his declining years? Olympian status and serenity, an overall view of world affairs, a seat in the House of Lords from which he could occasionally deliver the wise and weighty pronouncements of an elder statesman, and, until death supervened, the warm autumnal sun of personal fame: wasn't that fate, which now seemed to fall into his lap, both logical and desirable?

Not to Churchill. In temperament he was still the same man at 70 as he had been at 30, 40, or 50. Inactivity was still his personal hell and an observer's role still as unbearable; leisure was synonymous with boredom; fame and fortune were no consolation. Defeat was still as painful as it had ever been, and his reaction to the initial shock was the same as in the old days: it only steeled his resolve.

The septuagenarian girded himself for another trek through the political wilderness and worked on his comeback from early 1946 onwards. Declining the offer of a dukedom, he remained in the House of Commons as leader of the Conservative opposition and premier-in-waiting. His account of the Second World War? He wrote that too, all six volumes of it, with effortless facility. Not only was he insatiable, he seemed indestructible.

The years 1946 to 1951 constitute a remarkable period in Churchill's life. They almost seem a variation on the most questionable, equivocal years in his political career, the inter-war period during which he gradually fell out with all the political parties and ran his political reputation down to zero. Almost, but not quite. No one could rob him of the memory of 1940 or his renown as the victor of the Second World War, which soon passed into legend, and which he himself occasionally refurbished with great speeches in which the old lion and international statesman made himself heard once more, for instance at Fulton and Zurich in 1946, Amsterdam in 1948, and Strasbourg in 1949.

But was it fortuitous that all these speeches were delivered abroad? In London, during everyday parliamentary business, Churchill was not his wartime self but the Churchill of the 1920s: the reactionary, the polemicist, the headstrong, sometimes brilliant but frequently stubborn and inflexible party politician who made enemies and often caused his friends to shake their heads. He was fundamentally as little

Beware, for the time may be short. A shadow has fallen across the scenes so lately lighted by the Allied victory. Nobody knows what Soviet Russia and its Communist international organization intend to do in the immediate future. From Stettin in the Baltic to Trieste in the Adriatic an Iron Curtain has descended across the Continent.

WINSTON CHURCHILL, 1946

attached as he had ever been to the Conservative Party whose leadership he clung to almost out of spite. It was simply the steed that would carry him to his goal once more. The Conservatives, who naturally sensed this, often yearned to be rid of him, but he was not to be unseated. As for the Labour Party, which barred his return to power, he fought it with such ruthless, trenchant rigour and asperity that it was as if it had never supplied his principal wartime associates and comrades-in-arms. Churchill's periodic fits of magnanimity, during which he suddenly re-emerged as a statesman transcending party politics, were productive more of bewilderment than reconciliation.

No one would claim that Churchill's leadership of the Opposition was one of his greatest political achievements, or that it was he who eventually caused the Labour government to fall. Time

Bevin, Attlee and Morrison

took care of that. It wore the Labour government down just as it wears all governments down. But time is impartial. Churchill was subject to the same attrition. When he actually resumed the premiership at the head of a slender Conservative majority after the general election of October 1951 – an eventuality no one had really expected – people suddenly noticed what they had hitherto been tactful enough to ignore: that he was now an old man.

Although he had surmounted the excessive strains and exertions of the war years, he was six years older. He seemed to have become a trifle milder; his humanity and sense of humour had returned. There were occasional flashes of the old wit, and the lion would sometimes unsheathe its claws, but his hearing, for instance, had unmistakably deteriorated. His memory was also deteriorating: he could no longer recall the faces of the younger and more junior MPs, and even of his ministers, whom he sometimes got mixed up. He had become an enthusiastic reader of novels during his years of semi-leisure, a pastime from which he couldn't entirely desist even now that he was back in office. Reading novels is time-consuming, so the business of government tended to suffer in consequence. In the summer of 1949, while he was holidaying on the Riviera and thus out of the public eye, he suffered his first minor stroke. Although there were no perceptible after-effects, he had not regained his full capacity for work and powers of concentration. This became apparent when they were needed once more. Even in 1952, the first year of his new term, London insiders took to calling him a 'part-time premier', and by the end of that year a mood of resignation and disappointment had become rife. The days of Churchill's great achievements seemed over at last.

And then, after all, a new development occurred. Once more, and for the last time, the old giant drew himself up to his full height. For one brief moment, as in 1940, Churchill again became the cynosure of the entire world. It was a moment of hope, even though that hope remained unfulfilled.

It started early in 1953, when Anthony Eden, his long-time Foreign Secretary and successor designate, became gravely ill and was out of action for months. Strangely enough, this seemed to reinvigorate Churchill. He took over the Foreign Office while Eden was away, and the additional burden noticeably rejuvenated him. It was years since anyone had seen him in such good form. He was suddenly back in his element – almost as if it had only just occurred to him why he had remained in harness all this time and what he had still intended to do.

Anthony Eden (1897–1977), Conservative MP for Warwick and Leamington, served as Prime Minister from 1955 to 1957. A critic of appeasement, he served as Foreign Secretary in Churchill's wartime coalition, a position he again filled in 1951. In 1955 he succeeded Churchill as party leader and Prime Minister. His handling of the Suez Crisis in 1956 ruined his career. He resigned from office the following year.

For, over and above his many party-political activities, he had never rid himself of the tormenting sense that his real work had been cut short in 1945. Victory

Halifax and Eden

was complete, but nothing else: neither the permanent link with America that should have cushioned Britain's weakness and staunched her economic wounds, nor the restoration and pacification of Europe. War with Germany had been almost immediately superseded by the Cold War – not without Churchill's personal assistance. In 1945 he had probably hoped to use the new conflict as a means of furthering Anglo-American unification and supplementing it with a process of European unification: that had been the keynote of his celebrated speeches at Fulton and Zurich in 1946. But no one knew better than Churchill how blunt a weapon were the speeches of a man devoid of power. In America and Europe alike, his listeners heard only what they wanted to hear, not what really mattered to him. The Cold War had acquired a momentum of its own, however. Now that fighting had broken out in Korea, it threatened to escalate into a new world war without doing much to further the unification of the English-speaking peoples or that of Europe.

Meanwhile, Russia had also acquired the atomic bomb and both sides were busy developing the hydrogen bomb. Churchill the warrior realized, sooner than others, that war had now become impossible – it was time to make peace. He thought hard during those months. Capable of changing his mind once more, he envisioned the rough outlines of something akin to a new world order.

The Korean War began in 1950 when the Communist north invaded the non-Communist south. The south, aided by UN forces, then pushed Communist forces back to the Chinese frontier, whereupon China entered the fray. The conflict ended in 1953 with a return to the status quo ante.

And then Stalin died. This lent Churchill the final impetus. On 11 May 1953 he delivered the most astonishing speech of his life. Without warning or preparation, he altered the course that Britain and the West had been steering for seven years and – in effect – proclaimed the end of the Cold War. He proposed a summit conference with Stalin's successors and injected the word 'Locarno' into the debate – the notion of substituting a pan-European security system for opposing allied blocs.

The note Churchill struck on 11 May 1953 has resonated in international politics ever since. What he said then does not sound unfamiliar today, but he was the first to say it. At the time, in the thick of the Cold War, it shook the world. The Russians pricked up their ears, the Germans were startled, the Americans evinced surprise and concern.

The Locarno Pact. The international treaty signed at Locarno, Italy, in October 1925 agreed the post-war frontiers of France, Belgium, and Germany, and the demilitarization of the Rhineland. It was guaranteed by Italy and Britain. Locarno was part of the normalization of Germany's post-war relations with Western Europe, but was ominously silent about her eastern frontier.

The British experienced a sudden resurgence of hope – and pride. At a stroke, their grand old man had propelled them into the centre of the world stage. Churchill's peace plan was the last great international initiative to emanate from Britain.

But could it be called a plan, or did it consist of mere rudimentary, fragmentary ideas, massive components that did not fit together? It is hard to tell. Like certain late sketches by Rembrandt and Beethoven, this last great, late initiative of Churchill's inspires a feeling that it would, had he carried it through, have been the greatest of all his achievements. All the same, one doubts that he could ever have done so. Churchill aspired to many things that seemed incompatible: Anglo-American and European unification, and, transcending all else, universal atomic peace sustained by the re-establishment of the coalition that had won the Second World War. Perhaps they were simultaneously unattainable; perhaps the parts were incompatible with the whole. On the other hand, the products of statecraft can never, like other works of art, be harmoniously consummated and brought to a state of rigid perfection. Politics is in flux; all one can do is set things in motion and guide them in the hoped-for direction. And it cannot be denied that old Churchill set things in motion – violent motion – once more.

He was not permitted to guide them, however. He never again attained the summit – in more than one sense. Even before he reached the first stage – a preliminary summit conference between the Western powers, which he had pushed through in his initial élan, and at which he planned to recruit the Americans as partners in his new great game – he suffered another stroke.

On 27 June 1953 the British newspapers carried a special announcement: the Prime Minister was overworked and would have to take a month's leave from his duties. Overworked? A month off? That sounded quite unlike Churchill. In fact, he was confined to Chartwell, his country home, paralysed down one side and speaking with difficulty. His colleagues expected him to retire before long, his doctors thought he would soon be dead.

They had reckoned without his mental resilience and tough

Winston and Clementine Churchill at the British Embassy in Rome after his audience with Pope Pius XII in 1944

constitution. He did not give up – he never gave up. He was soon talking again about the summit conference, which was now to be held in September. *I feel, Charles,* he confided to his personal physician, *I could do something that no one else can do . . . Not perhaps world peace, but world easement. I feel I could change the bias of the world. America is very powerful, but very clumsy.*

All he could do at first was try to regain control of his body. The old international statesman had become a little child learning to walk – and childishly proud of the progress he was making. *I could not at present conduct the affairs of the government of the country. That is obvious,* he said on 19 July, his speech still slurred, *yet the physical recovery is good.* His doctor continues: 'He threw his legs out of bed and walked to the bathroom to demonstrate how much better his walking was. In the bathroom a bar had been put by the side of the bath; grasping this, he stepped into the empty bath and then proceeded to lever himself down till he sat in triumph, with only his silk vest on his person.' *I couldn't have done that a week ago,* he boasted.

And then, almost in the same breath: *Of course, the Russians may refuse to attend a conference* [at Stockholm] *on these terms. They would like me to visit them, I think, to spite America – not that I would ever split from the Americans.*

A few days later: *I feel there is a small bit of the brain which has been affected by this business and may, if I use it too much, crack . . . I don't like being kicked out till I've had a shot at this Russian business . . . I'm playing a big hand . . . If it came off, and there was disarmament . . . production might be doubled and we might be able to give to the working man what he has never had – leisure. A four-day week, and then three days' fun.*

He was constantly tormented by the notion that everything was being botched in his absence. Sometimes he burst into tears. *I was always a little blubbery, but now when I read anything, it moves me . . . Can't something be done about it?* Everything had gone wrong at the foreign ministers' conference held in lieu of the Western summit talks, and US Secretary of State and staunch Cold War warrior John Foster Dulles (1888–1959) had won the day. Dulles, said Churchill, was *clever enough to be stupid on a rather large scale*.

Churchill was still in a wheelchair at this time, but four weeks later he was once more walking with a stick, and in October at the Conservative Party Conference he delivered the first speech since his illness. It was an incredible triumph of willpower, but he was more nervous before that speech than he had ever been in his life. Although he had regained control of his body, his movements were still laboured. He often stumbled over his words and was unsure of his ability to remain on his feet for an hour at a stretch. He knew, however, that no one could be allowed to detect the slightest change in him: too many rumours had been circulating, and too many of his colleagues were expecting him to retire. Any sign that he had failed to make a full recovery and was not his old self again, any faltering or straying from his theme, let alone a physical collapse, would be the end of him. Churchill embarked on his speech like a man going into battle – a battle he won.

But it was all to no avail. He had missed his great moment, had lost his vital primary momentum and failed to reach the summit. Other matters thrust themselves to the fore. France's Indo-China crisis intervened, as did the Berlin situation and the foreign ministers' conference at Geneva. It was not until July 1954 that Churchill could finally revert to his great plan. He flew to America and reconnoitred the terrain, then wrote to Moscow proposing a two-power meeting. It was his last and boldest throw of the dice. He now risked something he had never risked in wartime: severance or apparent severance from the United States, a lone initiative – even, perhaps, a tacit threat to breach the alliance. If he could not persuade the Americans, he seemed prepared to constrain them. He wrote to Moscow privately, without consulting the Cabinet, just as he had always written privately to Roosevelt during the war.

But this time the Cabinet rebelled. The latitude his ministers had granted the wartime Prime Minister they would no long concede to Churchill on the threshold of 80, and he no longer had the strength to override them. How could he have done so? By threatening to resign? They were expecting his resignation in any case.

The truth was, they were not only expecting but pressing for it. And could the Conservatives really be blamed on that account? It was quite obvious by 1954 that Churchill was no longer physically equal to his duties. The euphoria of the first six months of 1953 had been a last flare-up – even, perhaps, a deceptive prelude to his final collapse. His recovery was heroic but incomplete; he had ceased to be even a part-time premier. One of his secretaries reported in confidence that he could be in great form for hours – better than ever, in fact. But then, suddenly, it was over, and for long periods he would simply be elsewhere in spirit.

He now suffered from the fits of depression that had very occasionally troubled him in the past. A legacy from his father's side of the family, they now became more frequent. *The Black Dog*, he called it: *The Black Dog is back.* His resistance weakened. When both of his most faithful supporters, Eden and Macmillan, urged him in turn to step down, he eventually gave way. That was early in 1955. He hesitated yet again, but on 5 April he really did resign. The London newspapers were on strike, so there were no valedictory articles. For the first time in his life, Churchill made no headlines.

In other respects, everything went off splendidly. His eightieth birthday had been celebrated unlike that of any living politician, and Elizabeth II (*b.*1926) was his guest at dinner the night before he left office – an unprecedented honour. Wearing court dress complete with knee-breeches, he opened the car door for her when she left. The street was crowded, flashguns lit up the spring night, cameras whirred. The old man bore himself magnificently: he smiled, in fact he almost seemed to beam. This time he had not been ousted: he was making a dignified exit showered with honours, apparently of his own free will. It was the first occasion on which he had left office in this manner, but this time it was a last farewell. Farewell to politics, to power, to his unfinished business. He felt that he was taking leave of life itself.

He lived on for nearly ten years of which there is nothing to be said. He entered upon them in bitterness. The bitterness gave way to melancholy and boredom, the boredom to gradual extinction.

Bitterness . . . However honourable and ostensibly voluntary his departure had been, to him it seemed no different from his three involuntary departures in the past. He had been repudiated and banished, this time finally and for good. He accepted the fact, but he could not take it lightly. He again declined the offer of a dukedom. Twice more, in 1955 and 1959, he stood for election to the

Churchill and Clementine Churchill bid farewell to the Queen and the Duke of Edinburgh, after a dinner at No 10 Downing Street shortly before his resignation in April 1955

BITTER YEARS

Churchill painting in the grounds of the Villa La Pausa at Roquebrune in the South of France

House of Commons, where, to begin with, he often occupied his former place – the corner seat beside the central aisle traditionally reserved for prominent independents and party rebels. But he no longer spoke. There were times when everyone expected him to do so, for instance after the Suez *débâcle* in October 1956. But he remained silent. He had decided to remain silent for evermore.

In the early years of his semi-retirement he still saw old friends, travelled, painted, read. Then, one by one, he abandoned these activities. He became very deaf, developed a number of geriatric complaints, and suffered several more strokes of varying severity. His menservants – he had always employed menservants – gradually became male nurses. He was carried up and down stairs, spent long summer hours in his garden and long winter hours in front of the fire, sometimes deep in thought, or so it seemed, and sometimes staring blankly into space or drawing in the sand with his stick.

Gradually, as the years went by, his failure to die became noticeable. At first he had often yearned for death because his useless existence had become a burden to him. But he couldn't die. He had never been able to give up. There was obviously something inside him that refused to give up even now – something which, whether or not he still realized it, was resisting to the last, resisting the death that was gradually taking possession of him just as he had resisted all his enemies in the past.

In 1962 he slipped and broke his thigh. By then he was 88, an age at which few survive such mishaps. Every newspaper got ready to print Churchill obituaries, and the finishing touches were put to the elaborate obsequies in preparation for him. He lay in plaster for two months. Then he was carried out of the hospital, shrunken, decrepit and almost unrecognizable – but still alive, still indomitable. A devoutly curious crowd was waiting outside, half moved, half sheepish, to greet the legendary figure who was still, incomprehensibly, alive. To many of the younger bystanders it seemed almost incredible that he had ever existed. The man who had made world history amid the flames of London in 1940 was almost as remote from them as the man who had taken part in Britain's last cavalry charge at Omdurman in 1898. Had he ever existed? Did he really still exist? Sure enough, there he was, being carried outside. He heard a timid cheer and essayed a feeble smile. He also raised his arm a little and splayed two fingers in the air to form the 'V for Victory' sign that had been his trademark in the war.

Even then, he lived on for quite a while. He died on 24 January 1965, in his ninety-first year, after a long final struggle with death. The street outside his home had again been thronged with people throughout the two weeks he lay in a coma. Many of them had lingered there for hours with solemn faces, like guests at a premature wake. The last words anyone heard him utter were: *It's all so boring.*

Britain gave him a magnificent funeral. One might have thought that it was not a man who was being borne to his grave, but British

The gun-carriage bearing Churchill's coffin at his State Funeral processes from Westminster Hall to St Paul's Cathedral in January 1965

Churchill's grave at Bladon Church

history itself – a resplendent, fortunate history whose last illustrious chapter Churchill himself had written almost a quarter of a century before. Everyone would gladly have seen him buried in Westminster Abbey or beside Nelson and Wellington in St Paul's Cathedral, but that he had forbidden. In the end, naval pallbearers carried his coffin down to the Thames Embankment, whence it was conveyed upstream by boat and then by train across country to the village of Bladon in Oxfordshire. And there, in accordance with his wishes, he was laid to rest in the obscure country churchyard where his father, too, lay buried.

Winston Churchill

Chronology

Year	Age	Life
1874		30 November: Winston Churchill born at Blenheim Palace
1876–9		Childhood in Dublin
1881–92		Schooldays at Ascot, Brighton, and Harrow
1893–4		Cadetship at Sandhurst
1895	20 21	January: his father dies. March: gazetted to the 4th Hussars November: war correspondent in Cuba
1896	22	India: polo and self-education
1897	23	Sees action on the North-West Frontier
1898	24	Takes part in the Sudan expedition; Battle of Omdurman

Year	History	Culture
1874	Disraeli succeeds Gladstone as Prime Minister.	Thomas Hardy, *Far from the Madding Crowd*.
1876–9	1876: Bell invents the telephone; Custer's last stand; Queen Victoria declared Empress of India. 1877: Edison and Swan produce first electric light. 1879: Zulu War.	1879: Henrik Ibsen, *A Doll's House*. Henry James, *Daisy Miller*.
1881–92	1881: Revolt of the Mahdi in the Sudan. 1886: Daimler produces his first motor car. 1887: Queen Victoria's Jubilee.	1881: Ibsen, *Ghosts*. James, *Washington Square* and *The Portrait of a Lady*. 1882: Richard Wagner, *Parsifal*. 1886: Robert Louis Stevenson, *Dr Jekyll and Mr Hyde*. 1890: James Frazer, *The Golden Bough*. Ibsen, *Hedda Gabler*. Émile Zola, *La Bête humaine*. 1891: Hardy, *Tess of the D'Urbervilles*. Rudyard Kipling, *Barrack-Room Ballads*. Oscar Wilde, *The Picture of Dorian Gray*.
1893–4	1894: Gladstone resigns; succeeded by Lord Rosebery. Dreyfus trial (1894–9) begins in Paris.	1893: Wilde, *Salome* published in Paris. Giuseppe Verdi, *Falstaff*. 1894: Kipling, *Jungle Book*. Algernon Charles Swinburne, *Astrophal and Other Poems*.
1895	Lord Rosebery resigns; succeeded by Lord Salisbury. Marconi invents 'wireless' transmission. Röntgen discovers X-rays. Freud's first published work on psychoanalysis.	Stephen Crane, *The Red Badge of Courage*. Hardy, *Jude the Obscure*. H G Wells, *The Time Machine*. Lumière brothers give first paying show of films in Paris.
1896	1 January: Jameson raiders defeated by Boers.	Anton Chekhov, *The Seagull*. A E Housman, *A Shropshire Lad*. Alfred Jarry, *Ubu roi*. Giacomo Puccini, *La Bohème*.
1897	22 June: Queen Victoria's Diamond Jubilee. Great Gold Rush begins.	James, *What Maisie Knew*. Stéphane Mallarmé, *Un Coup de dés*. Wells, *The Invisible Man*.
1898	2 September: Battle of Omdurman. The Curies discover radium. German naval expansion begins.	James, *The Turn of the Screw*. Wells, *The War of the Worlds*. Auguste Rodin, *Balzac*.

Year	Age	Life
1899	25	Leaves the army; stands unsuccessfully for Parliament; war correspondent in the Boer War; captured and escapes
1900	26	Recommissioned as an officer; serves in the Boer War. Elected to the Lower House
1904	30	Abandons the Conservative Party for the Liberal Party
1906	32	Under-Secretary of State for the Colonies
1908	34	President of the Board of Trade; marries Clementine Hozier
1910	36	Home Secretary
1911	37	October: First Lord of the Admiralty
1914	40	Defence of Antwerp; offers to resign

Year	History	Culture
1899	10 October: Boer War begins.	James, *The Awkward Age*. Arthur Symons, *The Symbolist Movement in Literature*. Wilde, *An Ideal Husband* and *The Importance of being Ernest*. W B Yeats, *The Wind among the Reeds*.
1900	6 January: Boers attack Ladysmith. 30 December: Australian Commonwealth proclaimed.	Joseph Conrad, *Lord Jim*. Jarry, *Ubu enchâiné*. Thomas Mann, *Buddenbrooks*. Friedrich Nietzsche, *Ecce Homo*. Puccini, *Tosca*.
1904	8 February: Russo-Japanese War begins.	Chekhov, *The Cherry Orchard*. Conrad, *Nostromo*. Puccini, *Madam Butterfly*. The Die Brücke group forms in Dresden.
1906	Movement for Women's Suffrage becomes active. Liberal Party wins land-slide majority in general election. Labour Party forms.	Robert Musil, *Young Törless*. Fauvism develops.
1908	Asquith's Old Age Pensions Plan.	E M Forster, *A Room with a View*. Gustav Mahler, *Das Lied von der Erde*. Cubism begins with Picasso and Braque.
1910	Liberal government retains office in two general elections. 6 May: Death of Edward VII; accession of George V.	Forster, *Howards End*. Rainer Maria Rilke, *Notebooks of Malte Laurids Brigge*. Igor Stravinsky's *The Fire Bird*.
1911	Parliament Act curtails power of House of Lords, establishes five-yearly elections. Lloyd George's National Insurance Act. Moroccan crisis. Chinese Revolution.	Conrad, *Under Western Eyes*. Mann, *Death in Venice*. Ezra Pound, *Canzoni*. Der Blaue Reiter group forms in Munich.
1914	28 June: Assassination of Archduke Ferdinand in Sarajevo. 28 July: Austria-Hungary declares war on Serbia. 1 August: Germany declares war against Russia. 3 August: Germany declares war on France. 4 August: German invasion of Belgium: Great Britain declares war on Germany. 12 August: Great Britain declares war on Austria-Hungary. 23 August: Battle of Mons. Japan declares war on Germany. 5–9 September: Battle of the Marne. 5 November: Great Britain declares war on Turkey. 17 December: British protectorate over Egypt proclaimed.	James Joyce, *Dubliners*. Pound, *Des Imagistes*.

Year	Age	Life
1915	41	18 May: dismissed as First Lord of the Admiralty; Chancellor of the Duchy of Lancaster. November: resigns; commands battalion in Flanders
1916	42	May: returns to the House of Commons
1917	43	Minister of Munitions
1919	45	Secretary of State for War and Minister of Air
1922	48	October/November: the Government falls; loses his seat
1924	50	Abandons the Liberal Party to rejoin the Conservative Party. November: Chancellor of the Exchequer
1929	55	The Government falls
1930	56	Resigns from the Conservative shadow cabinet

Year	History	Culture
1915	22 March: Naval attack on Dardanelles called off. 22 May: Italy declares war on Austria. 26 May: British coalition government formed. 20 August: Italy declares war on Turkey.	Franz Kafka, *Metamorphosis*. D H Lawrence, *The Rainbow*. Virginia Woolf, *The Voyage Out*.
1916	24 April: Republican rising in Dublin. 1 July–13 November: Battle of the Somme. 31 May: Battle of Jutland. 6 December: Lloyd George succeeds Asquith as Prime Minister and forms War Cabinet.	Guillaume Apollinaire, *Le poète assassiné*. Joyce, *A Portrait of the Artist as a Young Man*. G B Shaw, *Pygmalion*. Dada launched in Zurich with Cabaret Voltaire.
1917	6 April: United States declares war on Germany. 15 September: Russia proclaimed a republic. 7 November: Bolshevik Revolution. 8 November: Balfour declaration recognizes Palestine as 'a national home' for the Jews. 15 December: Russo-German armistice signed.	Apollinaire, *Les Mamelles de Tirésias* performed. T S Eliot, *Prufrock*. Lawrence, *Look! We Have Come Through!* Yeats, *The Wild Swans at Coole*.
1919	28 June: Treaty of Peace with Germany signed at Versailles. 10 September: Break-up of Austrian Empire. Einstein's Theory of Relativity experimentally confirmed. J M Keynes's The Economic Consequences of the Peace.	Kafka, *In the Penal Colony*. The Bauhaus founded in Weimar. United Artists formed with Charlie Chaplin, Mary Pickford, Douglas Fairbanks, and D W Griffith as partners.
1922	Fall of Lloyd George. Bonar Law heads Conservative government. 28 October: Mussolini's Fascist 'March on Rome'.	Eliot, *The Waste Land*. Joyce, *Ulysses*. Lawrence, *Aaron's Rod*. Osip Mandelstam, *Tristia*.
1924	January: MacDonald leads first Labour government. November: Conservative Party returns to office under Baldwin.	André Breton, First Surrealist Manifesto. Forster, *A Passage to India*. Kafka, *The Hunger Artist*. Mann, *The Magic Mountain*. Herman Melville, *Billy Budd*.
1929	MacDonald leads second Labour government. Wall Street crash.	Bertolt Brecht, *The Threepenny Opera*. Jean Cocteau, *Les Enfants terribles*. William Faulkner, *The Sound and the Fury*. Woolf, *A Room of One's Own*. Salvador Dali and Luis Buñuel, *Un Chien andalou*.
1930	Extreme parties (Communist and Nazis) win German elections: no majority can be found to form a government. London Maritime Disarmament Conference. Gandhi rebels against British Salt Monopoly and is imprisoned: first round-table talks in London without a Congress Party representative	W H Auden, *Poems*. Eliot, 'Ash Wednesday'. Faulkner, *As I Lay Dying*. Musil, *The Man without Qualities I*. Evelyn Waugh, *Vile Bodies*.

Year	Age	Life
1939	65	3 September: reappointed First Lord of the Admiralty
1940	66	10 May: Succeeds Chamberlain as Prime Minister and Minister of Defence
1943	69	November: Teheran Conference
1945	70	February: Attends Yalta Conference. May: end of the war in Europe and of the coalition government; stays on as Conservative Prime Minister. July: Conservative Party defeated at the general election

Year	History	Culture
1939	May–September: Battle of Nomonhan between Japan and USSR. 1 September: Germans invade Poland. 3 September : Great Britain and France declare war on Germany. 17 September: USSR invades Poland. 30 November: USSR invades Finland.	Joyce, *Finnegans Wake*. Yeats, *Last Poems*.
1940	12 March: Finland capitulates. 9 April: Germany invades Denmark and Norway. 10 May: Germans invade Low Countries and France. 20 May: Germans reach English Channel. 28 May: Belgium capitulates. 27 May–4 June: Dunkirk. 10 June: Italy declares war. 10 July–15 September: Battle of Britain. 27 September: Tripartite Pact between Japan, Germany, and Italy. 5 November: Roosevelt re-elected US President.	Graham Greene, *The Power and the Glory*. Ernest Hemingway, *For Whom the Bell Tolls*.
1943	2 February: Germans surrender at Stalingrad. 19 April–16 May: Rising and extinction of Warsaw Ghetto. 12 May: German-Italian surrender in Tunisia. 10 July: Allied invasion of Sicily. 3 September: Allied invasion of Calabria and signing of Italian surrender.	Eliot, *The Four Quartets*.
1945	12 January: General Russian offensive begins. 17 January: Russians enter Warsaw. 4–12 February: Yalta Conference. 13–14 February: Dresden raids. 12 April: Death of Roosevelt. 13 April: Russians enter Vienna. 16 April: Last Russian offensive begins. 28 April: Death of Mussolini. 30 April: Death of Hitler. 2 May: Berlin in Russian hands. 7 May: Germans surrender at Rheims. 9 May: Russians enter Prague. 17 July: Potsdam Conference. 26 July: Labour Party wins general election; Clement Attlee becomes Prime Minister. 6 August: Atomic bomb destroys Hiroshima. 14 August: Unconditional surrender of Japan. 27 December: IMF and World Bank established.	Benjamin Britten, *Peter Grimes*. Waugh, *Brideshead Revisited*.

Year	Age	Life
1945–51		Leader of the Conservative Opposition
1951	76	October: becomes Prime Minister again
1953	78	Major stroke; awarded the Nobel Prize for Literature
1955	79	5 April: resigns
1965	90	24 January: dies in London.

Year	History	Culture
1945–51	1946: Nuremberg sentences carried out: Goering's suicide. 1947: Lord Mountbatten last Viceroy of India. 'Marshall Plan' inaugurated. India and Pakistan independent after partition. 1948: Communists seize power in Czechoslovakia. British mandate in Palestine ends: new State of Israel proclaimed. Harry S Truman elected as US President. 1949: Republic of Ireland proclaimed. Federal Republic of Germany proclaimed. People's Republic of China proclaimed under Chairman Mao Zedong. German Democratic Republic proclaimed in Soviet sector. 1950: Indian republic proclaimed under President Rajendra Prasad. Labour Party wins general election. North Korea invades South Korea. China invades Tibet.	1947: Antonin Artaud, *Van Gogh, The Man Suicided by Society*. Mann, *Dr Faustus*. 1948: Greene, *The Heart of the Matter*. 1949: George Orwell, *Nineteen Eighty-Four*.
1951	Festival of Britain. Conservative Party defeats Labour Party in general election.	John Cage, *Music of Changes*. Karlheinz Stockhausen, *Kreuzspiel*.
1953	5 March: Death of Stalin. 29 May: Hillary and Tensing climb Mt Everest. 2 June: Elizabeth II crowned. July: Korean armistice signed.	William Burroughs, *Junkie*. First performance in Paris of Samuel Beckett's *Waiting for Godot*.
1955	Eden becomes Prime Minister. Conservative Party wins general election.	Vladimir Nabokov, *Lolita*. Waugh, *Officers and Gentlemen*.
1965	Vietnam War and anti-war protests. Soviet cosmonaut makes first space walk. Edward Heath new Conservative Party leader (but Harold Wilson's Labour Party in government). President de Gaulle re-elected in France.	Joe Orton, *Loot*. John Osborne, *A Patriot for Me*. Beckett, *Film* (with Buster Keaton) first shown in New York.

Further Reading

Even before his death, Sir Winston Churchill was already the subject of many books. There were more than a dozen biographies, most having appeared after his appointment as Prime Minister in May 1940. Lewis Broad, a popular biographer who chronicled the lives of many contemporary British politicians, produced a life of Churchill in 1940 that was constantly reprinted and became the standard life for a quarter of a century. In 1963–4 he extended his *Winston Churchill* to two volumes. An earlier, multi-volume biography published by Thames & Hudson in 1961 (written by Peter de Mendelssohn) got no further than 1911; a second volume never appeared. Most of these Lives were positive and were constructed largely from Churchill's own writings and speeches. There were several illustrated accounts of his life, notably *Churchill: His Life in Photographs* (1955) by his son, Randolph. There was by the time of his death little serious academic study of Churchill's life and career. Historians were denied access to the historical raw material as archives were governed by a 50-year rule (only relaxed by the first Wilson government) and access to state papers even within these tight confines was severely restricted. One particular essay has stood the test of time, however, and is worth revisting: Sir Isaiah Berlin's *Mr Churchill in 1940* (1949; reprinted in *Personal Impressions*, 1998).

The liveliest work was written by individuals highly critical of Churchill, most notably *Winston Churchill in War and Peace* (1950, revised 1955) by Labour MP Emmet Hughes. Trumbull Higgins's *Winston Churchill and the Second Front* (1957) identified Churchill's imperial mentality as an impediment to Allied success in the Second World War. Churchill's former chief link with the world of espionage, Desmond Morton, supplied inside information designed to damage Churchill's image in *Assignment Churchill* (1957) and *The Yankee Marlborough* (1963). Higgins opened up another front in his account of *Winston Churchill and the Dardanelles* (1963), a recurring item in the Churchill critique. In retrospect, the most damaging works to appear in Churchill's lifetime were the diaries of Sir Alan Brooke, Chief of the Imperial General Staff from 1941–5. Brooke's access to strategic planning gave an edge to his criticisms of Churchill. His diaries generated much controversy when they first appeared in two volumes during 1957–8, and Churchill tried very hard to prevent their publication. The complete edition – even more critical of Churchill than the versions that appeared in the 1950s – finally appeared as *War Diaries, 1939–45* (2001, edited by Alex Danchev and Daniel Todman).

In May 1960 Churchill gave his son permission to write his life. In 1962, ignoring the stipulation that he should begin this task only after his father's death, Randolph Churchill enlisted the services of Martin Gilbert, a research assistant from Oxford, to embark on a multi-volume life of *Winston S Churchill*. Volume I *Youth: 1874–1900* (1966), was the first book to be written about Churchill using his own papers – Randolph transferred his father's enormous personal archive to his home in Suffolk. Randolph's death in 1968 – after Volume II *Young Statesman: 1901–14* (1967) – led to the appointment of Martin Gilbert as official biographer. Gilbert completed the narrative of Churchill's life in six further volumes: Volume III *Challenge of War: 1914–16* (1971); Volume IV *Stricken World: 1916–22* (1975); Volume V *Prophet of Truth: 1922–39* (1976); Volume VI *Finest Hour: 1939–41* (1983); Volume VII *Road to Victory: 1941–45* (1986); Volume VIII *Never Despair: 1945–65* (1988). He continued Randolph's practice of producing supporting documentation in companion volumes. At the time of writing, this companion series has only reached December 1940; fifteen volumes of Churchill documentation have appeared, but many more will be required to complete the task. Even without these companions, the *Guinness Book of World Records* lists the Churchill and Gilbert *Life* as the longest biography of any individual. Gilbert has produced a one-volume synthesis just under a thousand pages long, *Churchill: A Life* (1991); he has also told the story of this enterprise: *In Search of Churchill* (1994). It is unlikely that any other life will ever be chronicled in such meticulous detail. Gilbert also interviewed Churchill's contemporaries, providing scholars with an extraordinary amount of new material.

While Gilbert beavered away, the number of studies of Churchill declined. There had been a flurry of interest immediately after his death, but there were fewer Churchill biographies published than there had been in the 1940s and 1950s. The 1970s was a lean decade in Churchill studies, the only notable work being Robert Rhodes James's *Churchill: A Study in Failure, 1900–1939* (1970); a clever book by an historian who had already produced a biography of Churchill's father, it examined Churchill's political career before 1 September 1939. Rhodes James also produced an edition of Churchill's speeches in eight volumes: *Winston S Churchill: His*

Complete Speeches, 1897–1963 (1974). David Cannadine has made a selection of the speeches, *Blood, Toil, Tears, and Sweat: The Speeches of Winston Churchill* (1989, reissued 1990).

Mary Soames, Churchill's daughter, quickly emerged as the principal keeper of the flame. It is she who represents her father at great state occasions and she has also produced an acclaimed biography of her mother *Clementine Churchill* (1979). More recently she edited her parents' correspondence: *Speaking for Themselves: The Personal Letters of Winston and Clementine Churchill* (1998). Lady Soames has also published an account of her father as an artist, *Winston Churchill: His Life as a Painter* (1990). Several memoirs of Churchill had appeared during his lifetime, but most members of his close circle delayed publication until after his death. Churchill's doctor, Lord Moran, produced a candid diary, *Winston Churchill: The Struggle for Survival* (1966), which raised more than a few eyebrows among the British establishment. It remains a fascinating intimate portrait. Sir John Colville – a diplomat and courtier who was Churchill's private secretary at Number 10 during his two premierships – published an account of Churchill's circle in *The Churchillians* (1981). It was based on his diaries, which later appeared as *The Fringes of Power: Downing Street Diaries, 1939–1955* (1985). They provide an extremely balanced account of Churchill as Prime Minister and are also a terrific read as Colville's elegant prose is bewitching. However, an examination of his original diaries (now housed at Churchill College, Cambridge) reveals how carefully he selected from his material. Professor Warren Kimball edited the correspondence between Churchill and Roosevelt in three volumes, *Churchill and Roosevelt: The Complete Correspondence* (1984), an excellent work. Kimball has also produced a study of this key relationship, *Forged in War: Churchill, Roosevelt, and the Second World War* (1997), which complements David Stafford's comprehensively researched *Roosevelt and Churchill: Men of Secrets* (1999). Stafford focuses on secret intelligence as a force binding the two allies. Churchill's relationship with Stalin is less well chronicled, but David Carlton's *Churchill and the Soviet Union* (2000) offers some useful insights.

During the 1980s and 1990s there was a renewed interest in Churchill. A cycle of public celebrations of the anniversaries of the Second World War – beginning in 1985 with the fortieth anniversary of the end of the conflict and finishing ten years later with the more grandiose fiftieth anniversary – reawakened public interest in Churchill. His reputation also benefited from a new fashion for historical documentaries on television, many of which explored the Second World War. Margaret Thatcher's identification with Churchill, the Falklands War, and the ending of the Cold War also contributed to focus attention on Churchill as an heroic leader. This had a particular resonance in the United States.

Archivists achieved wonders in cataloguing a vast number of documents to provide material for historians to re-examine Churchill's life. The Churchill papers found a permanent home in Churchill College, the public institution established in 1960 by the nation as a continuing memorial to Britain's wartime leader. Since 1974 the bulk of Churchill's personal papers (more than 2,000 boxes) and many of those of his friends and collaborators have been housed in the Churchill Archive Centre. The entire Churchill collection can now be searched electronically and parts of the catalogue are available online (see www.chu.cam.ac.uk). The collection is also in the process of being microfilmed so that the Churchill papers will be available in libraries across the globe. It is a remarkable achievement, all the more so because it is the work of a small group of dedicated archivists working on a shoestring. The Churchill College Archives Centre should be the first point of departure for anyone embarking on a study of Sir Winston Churchill.

The archivists at the Public Records Office in Kew have matched this industry and each year they release more documentation on the age in which Churchill lived. The 1990s brought a more liberal attitude to the release of intelligence decrypts, a source that fascinated Churchill. David Stafford has shown the importance of this element in Churchill's career, while at the same time undermining many popular myths about Churchill in *Churchill and the Secret Service* (1997, new edn 1999).

The last three decades have been dominated by a succession of new single-volume biographies most of which are heavily indebted to Gilbert: Henry Pelling (1974), Elizabeth Longford (1974), Piers Brendon (1984), Richard Lamb (1991), Keith Robbins (1992), Norman Rose (1994), Robert Blake (1997), Roy Jenkins (2001) and Geoffrey Best (2001). All can be characterized as sound and reliable narratives generally favourably disposed to their subject.

There were even a few revisionist works. David Irving has thrown much mud in his indictment of Churchill as war leader in *Churchill's War: Volume 1, The Struggle for Power* (1981). It included some particularly novel sources of information, such as the citation 'Mrs Goering to the author'! Clive Ponting attacks Churchill in his *Churchill* (1994), which mobilized reviewers to denounce the former civil servant's political correctness. The biography is infuriatingly negative, but is worth reading simply because Ponting raises some very good points (which are sometimes lost among the relentless hostility). Ponting brought Churchill's racism (rooted in social Darwinism) to the foreground and with more detachment might have been able to explore this important subject so often neglected or dismissed by Churchill's biographers. Altogether more convincing are John Charmley's two excursions into revision, *Churchill: The End of Glory* (1993) and *Churchill's Grand Alliance* (1995). Charmley attacks from the Right, focusing on Churchill's culpability as destroyer of the British Empire and as a vassal to the Americans. Charmley is steeped in the sources and writes engagingly. Andrew Roberts, a young Thatcherite historian, also shows a formidable mastery of the sources in his lively debunking of the Churchill myths, *Eminent Churchillians* (1994). He adds many fresh charges to the revisionist indictment, including Churchill's contribution to – and responsibility for – British post-war economic underachievement.

In many ways, however, the more interesting work is being done elsewhere. The academic study of Churchill continues in earnest and provides not only fresh material but shifting perspectives on Sir Winston. The historical figure can be properly measured against his contemporaries; his ideas, policies, and decisions can be understood within the context of the time. Building on a seminal book – *The Road to 1945* (1975, reissued 1994), still the best introduction to the domestic impact of Churchill's wartime government – Professor Paul Addison has made many contributions to Churchill studies. His most important and most accessible work, *Churchill on the Home Front*, studies Churchill on the domestic scene from 1900–55; it is a brilliant book. Also of interest is his essay on 'The Search for Peace in Ireland' (in *Churchill as Peacemaker* (1997), edited by James Muller) which tells the story of Churchill's reaction to the creation of the Irish Free State. An earlier essay on 'The Political Beliefs of Winston Churchill' in *Transactions of the Royal Historical Society*, Fifth Series, Volume XXX (1980), pp 23–47, is still important for those seeking an understanding of Churchill's mind.

Dr David Reynolds, a prolific writer on Anglo-American relations, has produced several important essays on Churchill which engage with the evidence in a sophisticated and stimulating way: 'Churchill and the British "Decision" to Fight On in 1940: Right Policy, Wrong Reasons', in R Langhorne (ed) *Diplomacy and Intelligence during the Second World War* (1985) pp 147–67; 'Churchill the Appeaser? Between Hitler, Roosevelt, and Stalin in World War Two', in M L Dockrill and B J McKercher (eds) *Diplomacy and World Power: Studies in British Foreign Policy, 1890–1950* (1996) pp 197–220; and 'Churchill's Writing of History: Appeasement, Autobiography, and *The Gathering Storm*', in *Transactions of the Royal Historical Society*, Sixth Series, Volume XI (2001) pp 221–47. This last article is an instalment of a longer work examining Churchill's six-volume history of *The Second World War*, providing a perfect companion to Robin Prior's *Churchill's 'World Crisis' as History* (1983) about Churchill's earlier cycle of books on the Great War. These recent works tell us much about Churchill as writer, historian, and rhetorician.

Two doctoral studies (both produced at Cambridge) have been turned into fine books that deserve much attention. In *Burying Caesar* (1999) Graham Stewart cleverly converts his thesis on Churchill and the Conservative Party from 1929–37 into a fascinating account of the struggle between Neville Chamberlain and his political nemesis. Shelia Lawlor submitted her thesis a decade earlier but her account of decision-making at the top during 1940 and much of 1941, *Churchill and the Politics of Power* (1994), is superb and recommended.

Professor R Breitman provides fresh perspectives on the continuing controversy about Churchill and his knowledge of the Holocaust. Michael Cohen's *Churchill and the Jews* (1985) argues that Churchill could have done more to publicize the killings and made things more difficult for the German killers. Breitman's *Official Secrets: What the Nazis Planned, What the British and Americans Knew* (1998, reissued 2000) shows that intelligence sources, aware of Churchill's sympathies for the Jews (unusual among members of his class) kept significant intelligence decrypts from him.

A whole branch of military history has devoted itself to chronicling both the First and the Second World Wars. John Keegan has edited a collection of essays on *Churchill and the Generals* (1991) while Churchill's association with the Royal Navy is chronicled in Stephen Roskill's *Churchill and the Admirals* (1977). Both provide good introductions to the question of civil and military relations in mid-twentieth-century Britain.

Thirty-seven years after Churchill's death two trends can be discerned. The heroic Churchill dominates the popular mind, cultivated by politicians, journalists, documentary-makers, and nostalgic historians of an older generation, all eager to feed the national appetite for 'greatness'. This popular history is constructed around a strange Manicheism which pits the Good Leader (Churchill) against the Evil Leader (Hitler) in a titanic epic, providing contemporary resonances and legitimating much contemporary political activity, especially in the sphere of international relations. In Britain it mirrors a strong anti-German sentiment that has become increasingly prevalent in recent decades. The best example of this genre are two books by John Lukacs, *The Duel: Hitler vs Churchill: 10 May – 31 July 1940* (1990), and *Five Days in London, May 1940* (1999), polemical moral tracts that rest upon many dubious readings of the evidence. R A C Parker has even managed to produce a completely unconvincing book based on the premise that Churchill could have stopped the Second World War had he been given power in the 1930s, *Churchill and Appeasement* (2000). It is a splendid read, Parker's prose is a good deal more seductive and less angular than Lukacs's sermons – he is a much less angry old man. An enduring national attraction focusing on Churchill as war leader can be found in central London at the Cabinet War Rooms: the 'good' bunker, as it were, abandoned in 1945 but opened as a national monument in 1984 and now one of the most popular visitor attractions in the UK.

Alongside these heroic tales, academic historians have produced a more complex portrait of Winston Churchill as a human being. The fruits of one academic conference (published as *Churchill* (1993), edited by R Blake and W R Louis) and those of another held in London (published in the *Transactions of the Royal Historical Society*, Sixth Series, Volume XI, 2001) reveal the current state of academic thinking. Many contributions in both collections can be recommended, but Donald Cameron Watt's splendid account of 'Churchill and Appeasement' in the Blake and Louis volume is scholarship of the highest level – it might give even the myth-makers pause for thought.

There is a special Internet bookshop devoted to Churchilliana (www.churchillbooks.com), offering a range of items by and about Churchill at prices to suit all pockets. Professor Eugene Rasnor lists more than 3,000 books by and about Churchill in *Winston S Churchill 1874–1965: A Comprehensive Historiography and Annotated Bibliography* (2000).

PATRICK HIGGINS

May 2002

Picture Sources

The author and publisher wish to express their thanks to the following sources of illustrative material and/or permission to reproduce it:

Associated Press: pp. 143, 146; Broadwater Collection © Curtis Brown: pp. 4, 6, 15, 28, 138, 151, 156; Hulton Getty: pp. x, 18, 25, 76, 85, 90, 99, 127, 129, 136, 142, 148, 155; Imperial War Museum: pp. 119, 123, 125, 135, 140; Novosti: pp. 67, 80; Topham: pp. 35, 41, 50, 52, 64, 72, 82, 84, 87, 97, 105, 113

Index